1/23

LION

THE STORY OF THE REAL TITFIELD THUNDERBOLT

Anthony Dawson

AMBERLEY

Acknowledgements

In researching this history of perhaps one of the best-known steam locomotives, I would like to thank Sharon Brown and Dale Riley, of National Museums Liverpool, for access to records held by the museum as well as for being granted permission to survey *Lion*. Secondly, thanks must also go to John Brandrick of OLCO for access to archive material and drawings in their care, as well as for the use of photographs; and to those who provided illustrations including David Boydell, Paul Dore, Ian Hardman, Ben Jackson, Dr Rudi Newman and Tom Nicholls. Also, to Ted Talbot and to Dave Bond, Chairman of the L&NWR Society, for permission to reproduce images in their collection. Thanks also to Trevor Bates for sharing his memories and photographs of Lion at Rustons Diesels. Thanks, as ever, to the former MOSI Railway Volunteers for their friendship, and to Andy Mason for his continued support of my writing endeavours.

First published 2020

Amberley Publishing
The Hill, Stroud
Gloucestershire, GL5 4EP

www.amberley-books.com

Copyright © Anthony Dawson, 2020

The right of Anthony Dawson to be identified as the Author of this work has been asserted in accordance with the Copyright, Designs and Patents Act 1988.

ISBN 978 1 4456 8505 2 (print)
ISBN 978 1 4456 8506 9 (ebook)

British Library Cataloguing in Publication Data.
A catalogue record for this book is available from the British Library.

Origination by Amberley Publishing.
Printed in the UK.

Contents

Chapter 1

The Liverpool &
Manchester Railway

In order to understand the story of *Lion* we need to go back to 15 September 1830, some eight years before she was built. On that memorable, and somewhat damp, day the Liverpool & Manchester Railway – the world's first intercity, double-track, mainline railway – was opened by the Duke of Wellington. The railway had cost over £1 million and had been founded by two wealthy businessmen – Joseph Sandars of Liverpool and John Kennedy of Manchester – to revolutionise transport between those two industrial towns. It had taken six years of hard work to get an enabling Act through Parliament and then to build the line, under the direction of George Stephenson. Many naysayers said the line could never be built – that Stephenson would never get his railway across the morass of Chat Moss – or even more bizarrely cows would give sour milk, horses would go extinct

The opening day of the Liverpool & Manchester Railway on 15 September 1830, depicted by Isaac Shaw.

and birds fall from the sky. Much was made about the danger of the steam locomotive, and travel at the then unbelievably high speed of 20 mph. Despite this opposition, the railway was built and proved to be an immediate success, carrying over 6,000 passengers between the two towns during the first full week of operation.

The use of locomotives on the Liverpool & Manchester Railway, however, was not a foregone conclusion. Many on the Board of Directors were in favour of haulage via stationary engines and endless ropes, and despite having sought expert opinion from John Rastrick and James Walker, who carried out a tour of inspection of all the major railways then in existence (1828–1829), the 'jury was still out' over locomotive vs stationary engines. To this end, in April 1829 the Directors organised what became known as the 'Rainhill Trials' in order to ascertain whether the 'most improved' locomotive was as good as, or better than, winding engines and ropes. Of the 'multifarious schemes' suggested, ultimately four locomotives were entered into the trial in October 1829: *Rocket* by George and Robert Stephenson and Henry Booth, *Novelty* by John Braithwaite and John Ericsson, *Sans Pareil* by Timothy Hackworth and *Perseverance* by Timothy Burstall. As history records, *Rocket* was 'for blood and bone united', and 'by far the best engine' running without accident or mishap for 70 miles – admittedly in short 1½-mile bursts – the equivalent to a return trip from Liverpool to Manchester at an average speed of 15 mph, hauling a load of three times its own weight.

It was with locomotives based on the design of *Rocket* that the Liverpool & Manchester was opened. But what was needed was a faster, more powerful design of locomotive for the first regular timetabled mainline passenger and goods service to develop. That locomotive was *Planet*. Delivered on 4 October 1830, she was the progenitor of the 'modern' steam locomotive: a 2-2-0 with a multi-tubular boiler with the firebox within the boiler shell and a proper smokebox at the opposite end; cylinders set low down under the smokebox driving a crank axle; proper frames with horn guides and springs. On 23 November she

Planet was the first 'modern' locomotive, incorporating a boiler design with a firebox within the boiler shell, a proper smokebox and horizontal cylinders driving a crank axle. This replica was first steamed in 1992.

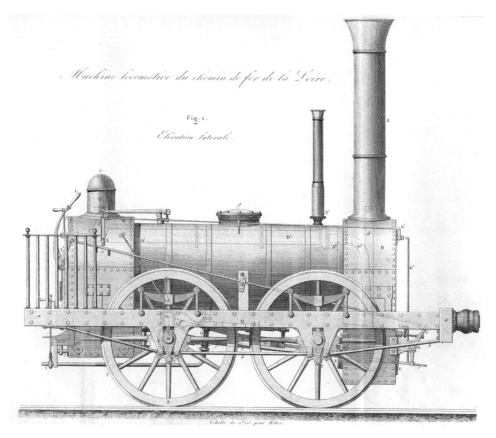

Machine locomotive du chemin de fer de la Loire.

Fig. 1.

Élévation latérale.

Échelle de 0.03 pour Mètre.

The natural development of the 2-2-0 Planet class was the 0-4-0 Samson class for working heavy goods trains.

made the run from Liverpool to Manchester in sixty minutes (including a stop of two minutes to oil round), making an average speed of 30 mph. Then, a week later, she made the same run with a load of 80 tons of merchandise (an unprecedented amount) at an average speed of 16 mph in two hours fifty-four minutes. Whilst *Planet* and her sixteen sisters inaugurated a fast passenger service between Liverpool and Manchester, an even more powerful locomotive was needed to operate a regular goods service – or as it was then called 'luggage' – leading to the development of the first purpose-built mainline goods engine: the 0-4-0 'Samson' class. *Samson* and her sister *Goliath* were delivered in spring 1831, and the performance of *Samson* 'completely threw into the shade' that of *Planet* only a few months before. In February 1831 she managed to handle a load of 151 tons, and whilst *Planet's* all-out effort of 80 tons in November 1830 had been a one-off, *Samson* was able to regularly haul loads of 60 tons of goods between the two towns. A further four 0-4-0 Samson class locomotives were delivered to the Liverpool & Manchester: *Atlas*, *Milo*, *Titan*, *Orion* and it is to these locomotives that *Lion* owes her design.

Growing Traffic

Goods traffic continued to grow, but this in itself presented two problems: trains had to be frequently double-headed and the lightly laid track was unable to cope with the weight of the locomotives. The track was laid with wrought-iron fish-bellied rails weighing 35 lbs per yard, secured with iron wedges to cast-iron chairs, which were secured to stone blocks 2 feet square. George Stephenson had estimated before the line opened that the track would be good for at least sixty or seventy years, but after less than a year of operation, with many rails and stone blocks breaking, it was clear that the track was simply not strong enough. It had been designed to support a maximum axle load of 4½ tons, and indeed the Liverpool & Manchester Act stipulated no rail-borne vehicle could weigh more than 4 tons loaded. Despite this, *Planet* had an axle load of 5 tons, and John Dixon, the Principal Engineer, reported to the Board that he was amazed as to how the 'very lightweight' 35 lb rail had 'carr[ied] the present Engines at the present velocities without being all ruined or spoilt in a week'. In order to reduce the axle load, George Stephenson recommended in May 1832 the use of a six-wheeled engine in order to spread the load over a greater area. In the meantime, the Board of Directors took the brave decision to re-lay with rails weighing 60 lb, and later 75 lb per yard, a process which was finished by the summer of 1838.

Thus, the idea of a six-wheeled locomotive was another logical development from *Planet*. The first six-wheelers on the Liverpool & Manchester were all conversions of existing locomotives: *Atlas* was rebuilt as an 0-4-2 in February 1832 and *Mercury* was modified to become a 2-2-2 in December 1833. *Titan* and *Orion* (0-4-0 Samson class engines) were also rebuilt as 0-4-2s, marking the start of the 'Large Samson' class of which *Lion* is a unique survivor. Thereafter, the six-wheeled 2-2-2 'coaching engines', for passenger duties, and the heavier 0-4-2 'luggage engines', for goods working, became the standard locomotive on the Liverpool & Manchester until the 1840s. But even after the introduction of more powerful six-wheeled engines, some heavy trains still required assistance up the Whiston and Sutton inclines of 1:96 and heavyweight 0-4-2 'bank' engines were ordered.

Lion and her sister, *Tiger*, were ordered by the Liverpool & Manchester Board in October 1837. Henry Booth, the line's general superintendent, had reported to the Board that given a predicted increase in traffic from 1837–1839, new 'luggage' and 'coaching' engines would be needed. He had approached several reputable locomotive builders and ten locomotives were ordered in October 1837 and four more in Spring 1838. The Management Committee resolved on 2 October 1837:

The treasurer stated that in conformity with the instructions of the Board he had contracted for Ten Locomotive Engines, viz. With Todd, Kitson & Laird of Leeds, for - 2 Luggage engines with 11-inch cylinder, 20-inch stroke to be delivered on the 30th April 1838 £1,100 each.
2 Coaching Engines with 11 ½-inch cylinder, 18-inch stroke. 5' 6" wheels. To be delivered on the 30th June for £1,060 each.
2 Bank Engines with 13-inch cylinder, 20-inch stroke, to be delivered 30th September 1838 for £1, 1130 each.

With Benjamin Hick of Bolton for -
2 Luggage engines. 11-inch cylinder, 20-inch stroke. To be delivered 30th June 1838 for £1,350 each.

With Rothwell & Co., for -
2 Coaching Engines. 11-inch cylinders, 18-inch stroke.
    1 to be delivered by the 31st May
    1 to be delivered by the 30th June 1838 for £1,250 each. (RAIL371/10, Minute 2 October 1837)

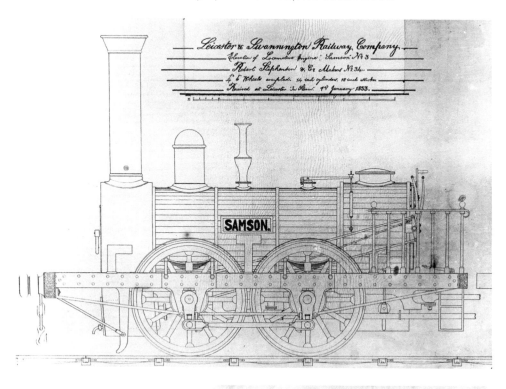

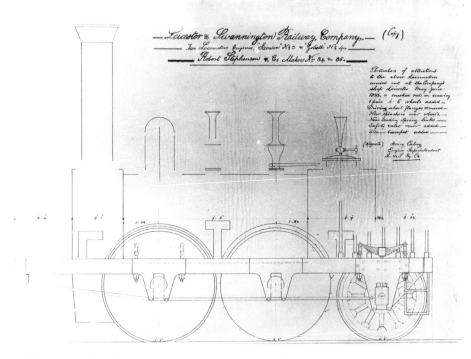

Above and opposite page: In order to reduce axle load to reduce track damage, the logical evolution of the Planet and Samson class was to add carrying wheels: take a 0-4-0 Samson and add a frame extension and pair of carrying wheels to create a 0-4-2 Large Samson, of which *Lion* is a member.

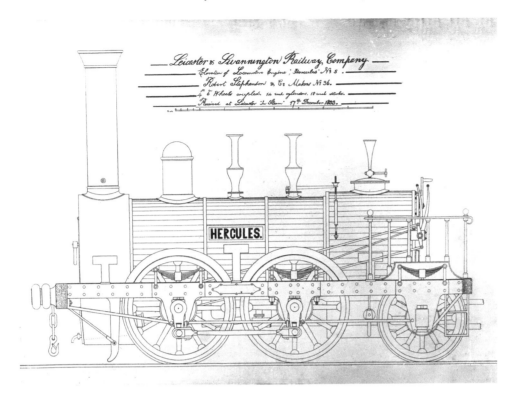

The six locomotives by Todd, Kitson & Laird were named *Lion* (57), *Tiger* (58), *Leopard* (62), *Panther* (64), *Elephant* (65), *Buffalo* (67); the two by Hick were *Samson* (66) and *Goliath* (68); whilst *Rokeby* (59) and *Roderick* (60) were built by Rothwells. They were built incorporating many of the 'patent improvements' designed by the railway's Locomotive Foreman, John Melling.

Lion is a typical member of the Stephenson six-wheeled 'luggage engine' of the 1830s. She has an outside 'sandwich frame' of oak (two lengths spliced together) sandwiched between wrought-iron plates, connected at the front and back with transoms and inside iron plate frames. The boiler assembly is considered to be the main structural element of the locomotive. It sits on three brackets which are bolted to the outside frames, and in turn are riveted to the boiler. Between the cylinders and firebox are a pair of inch-thick wrought-iron plate frames; these probably date from 1841 and originally *Lion*, like *Planet*, would have had four inside plate frames. The present set of inside frames are bolted to an angle mounted on the rear face of the cylinders. At the rear end, they are bolted to a T-shaped wrought-iron sub-frame which is bolted to the side of the firebox wrapper; the 'leg' of the T wraps around the front corner of the firebox wrapper. There are three pairs of redundant bolt holes on each frame. The inside frames help support the crank axle. In the days before James Nasmyth invented the steam hammer, it was difficult to forge a reliable crank axle by hand. Thus a 'belt and braces' approach was taken so that the crank axle had multiple sources of support. The crank axle is 5 ½ inches diameter, reducing to 4½ where it passes through the wheel and into the outside bearing, and is supported at each end in sprung bearings supported by the outside frame. There is a second set of sprung bearings on the inner frame so that the wheel is carried between each set of frames. The axle boxes are solid brass (with no white metal liner) and oil pots for wick lubrication.

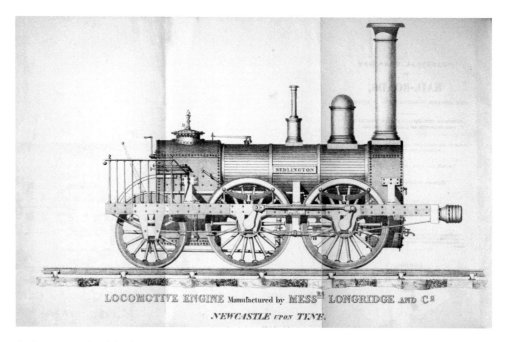

A classic example of the Stephenson Large Samson class, which was built by a number of manufacturers including Longridge & Co. in Beldington, Northumberland.

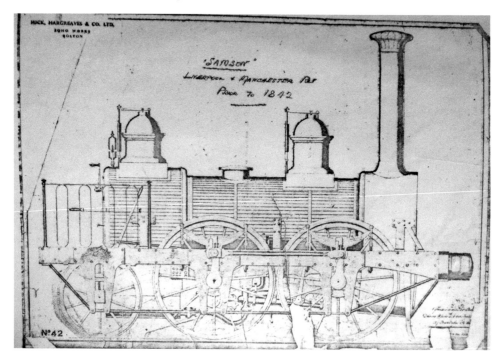

Samson was built by Hick, Hargreaves & Co. of Bolton as part of the same order and specification as *Lion*. She had 5-foot driving wheels, 3-foot 6-inch carrying wheels and cylinders 11 × 20 inches. *Lion* would have had a similar appearance to *Samson* when first built with two steam domes and a slightly raised outer firebox. (OLCO)

A rare photograph of a Large Samson at work, *c.* 1860s at the Hetton Colliery, near Newcastle. The 'stew pot' shape of the steam dome suggests it was built by Hawthorns.

View underneath *Lion* looking forward. The iron inner plate frames are visible on the left, as are the boiler support brackets which are riveted to the boiler and secure to the inner and outer (sandwich) frames. (OLCO)

Looking toward the cylinders, the 'spectacles', which support the ends of the slide bars, are readily visible. They are supported by brackets riveted to the boiler barrel. The valve gear has very minimal clearances. (OLCO)

Thus, in case of a crank axle failure the wheel would remain in an upright position and hopefully the locomotive would not derail. The leading wheels, which have a plain axle, are only supported via the outside frames. This is an evolution and simplification from the frame of the pioneering *Planet*, which had four inside frames that left very little room to accommodate the valve gear etc. beneath the locomotive. Whereas *Planet*'s slide bars were carried by the four inside frames, on *Lion* one end of the slide bar is secured to the cylinder end caps via tapered threaded studs, and, at the opposite, by wrought-iron 'spectacles', which are bracketed off the frame and supported from the boiler barrel.

John Melling

John Melling (1782–1856) of Wigan had been appointed 'Foreman of the Repairing Shops' at the Brickfield Station, near Edgehill in Liverpool, on the Liverpool & Manchester Railway in 1830; his colleague at the opposite end of the line in Manchester was Alexander Fyfe (*c.* 1790–1848). Melling's son, Thomas (1817–1896), worked as his assistant until 1837 when he moved to join the Grand Junction Railway as their locomotive superintendent. Following the dismissal of Anthony Harding as Locomotive Foreman (for gross misconduct) in April 1833, Melling assumed that mantle, and from 1837, with the focus on locomotive repair at the Liverpool end of the line at Edge Hill, became de facto Locomotive Superintendent in all but title.

John Melling was of an inventive turn of mind and presented several of his ideas to the Board of Directors for their perusal, including: a firebox with hollow, water-filled fire bars with a water tank underneath acting as a feed-water heater (1832); a hollow double

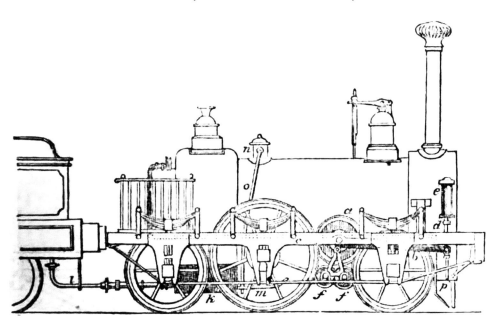

An extract from John Melling's Patent Application of 1838 showing the 'Coupling Wheel', which also acted as a brake, raised and lowered by a steam cylinder; his feed-water heater under the ash pan and cock was to direct waste steam back into the tank.

axle (1833), which allowed one wheel to rotate at a different speed to aid locomotives going around curves; and a steam-operated 'coupling wheel' (1833), which could be raised or lowered between the driving and carrying wheels of a locomotive to increase its adhesion. The Directors saw promise in these ideas and granted full-scale trials with his firebox and 'coupling wheel' ideas.

From 1837 Melling was able to give free reign to his ideas, for which he received letters patent in October of that year. Melling's Patent Application (No. 7410 of 26 July 1837) included six different inventions. The first was his 'Coupling Wheel' which did away with the need for outside coupling rods, and helped increase adhesion with a heavy load or when rails were 'in a wet or greasy state.' A third, smaller wheel, which could be raised or lowered via a steam cylinder, was placed between the driving and leading wheel. In its lowered position, it coupled both wheels together. Melling, rather like Patrick Stirling (1820–1895) of the Great Northern Railway forty years later, thought that coupling rods were 'undesirable' as they increased friction and therefore wear, and the 'hammer blow' effect of them damaged the track. Stirling famously remarked that coupled engines were 'like a laddie runnin' wi' his breeks doon'. Melling's 'coupling wheel' did away with the need for coupling rods, but also meant additional adhesion was available when required through the coupling of extra wheels. Melling noted that:

> The contrivance is very advantageous in comparison with the ordinary previous mode of coupling between any two wheels, because, if the rail be dry or the adhesion sufficient, the anti-friction wheel may be lifted off and remain idle, while the ordinary system of outside cranks and connecting rods must always continue working, and thus, at certain times, act as an incumbrance. Another important feature … is the smoothness with which the engine works … compared to engines coupled in the

ordinary manner. The improvement is affected by transmitting a considerable portion of the weight from the cranked or driving axle to the straight or independent axle, which entirely prevents the tremulous lateral motion of ordinary locomotive engines.

The wheels could thus be coupled or uncoupled at will, and 'at any rate of running'. The first locomotive to be so fitted was *Firefly*, in February 1837, and *Arrow*, in May 1837. Although seemingly 'Heath Robinson', Melling's 'coupling wheel' was an idea revived by Francis Webb, Chief Mechanical Engineer of the LNWR, in the 1880s.

Melling's second invention was similar: a brake which used two small wheels, which could be raised or lowered by steam between the driving wheel and another wheelset. As the two small wheels ran in opposite directions, a braking effect was produced. His third invention was using hollow water-filled firebars and a method of heating the feed water by placing a water tank underneath the firebars, 'The falling cinders from the furnace, as they are caught by this water ash-box, will heat the water therein.' The water from this tank was able to circulate with that in the tender tank via leather hoses, meaning that the tender water would be heated. Waste steam taken from the safety valve could also be turned via a special cock into the tender tank, helping to heat the feed water in the tank under the firebox. Water-filled firebars had been used by other engineers before (including George Stephenson), but because they quickly became fouled with scale and sludge were not a successful idea. A fifth was to use a steam jet 'for the purpose of cleansing the rails from snow, grease, or sand…'

His most successful innovation was his radial valve gear. Instead of using eccentrics to drive the valves, Melling derived it from a pin in the centre of the connecting rod working in a slotted link:

> Mr Melling … made a stud fast in the middle of the connecting rod, which by the nature of the connecting-rod motion, described a species of elliptical curve … The stud worked in a slot formed in a lever, of which this axis was placed in the centre of the oval. This arm the pin carried round with it, and on the same axis a small crank worked the valve-rod, like an ordinary eccentric. (Clark 1855: 23)

The 'small cranks' worked four gab-ended connecting rods, which, via a single lever on the footplate, could be simultaneously raised or lowered to engage or disengage with a pin on a rocker arm, providing fore or back gear.

The first locomotive to be fitted with Melling's valve gear was the Grand Junction engine *Lynx* in October 1837, but the Mellings (father and son) got into serious difficulty with the Directors of the Liverpool & Manchester and the Grand Junction. Whilst John Melling had recommended to the Liverpool & Manchester Board that they adopt his various improvements for their new locomotives, he not only failed to inform them he had in fact patented these improvements, but that he also expected a royalty payment! Suffice to say the L&M Board was not impressed when they found this out in December 1837. Melling was brought before the Board in January 1838 and severely reprimanded. Indeed, the Board suggested he sign a legal agreement with them for the use of his patents, but he refused. Eventually, Melling backed down and agreed that he would not charge the Liverpool & Manchester any royalties for as long as he was employed by them. The Board made a gift of 100 guineas to cover any royalties for the eleven engines then being built, and Melling agreed he would only charge his employers half the fee for further use of his inventions for as long as he was in their employ. Finally, in March 1838 the L&M Board agreed that Melling would be paid 50 guineas for the use of his 'patent improvements', and furthermore:

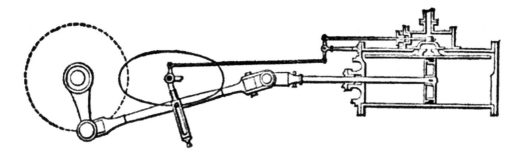

Melling's patent radial valve gear with which *Lion* was fitted when new. Movement for the valves was derived from a pin in the centre of the connecting rod which worked in a slotted link.

> That it would be desirable that when Engines had to undergo a thorough repair, they should be refitted with the patent improved gearing, the Charge for which this Company on the part of the Patentee was 50 Guineas an Engine, which would comprise (if it were thought proper to adopt them) the patent coupling wheel and the water tight ash pan. (RAIL 371/10, Minute 16 March 1838)

But this was not the end of the saga: Melling senior and junior had also attempted a similar ruse with the Directors of the Grand Junction. At the suggestion of Thomas Melling, the GJR had ordered ten locomotives fitted with his father's patent improvements but had also failed to inform them they were patented. The furious GJR Directors flatly refused to pay Melling's royalties of £52 per engine, and instead presented him with 200 guineas (twice what the L&M Directors had paid) for the ten engines built according to his patent! Eventually the GJR would own over twenty locomotives built to Melling's patent.

A list of locomotives drawn up by Melling and dated 10 April 1839 shows that some thirteen locomotives of the L&M fleet were fitted with his patent valve gear (*Lion* amongst them). The remaining L&M locomotives all used the 'old hand eccentric gear' as used on *Planet*.

The Leeds Lion

Lion was built by the Leeds firm of Todd, Kitson & Laird. The company had been formed on 1 September in a converted mill in Hunslet by James Kitson (1807–1885), who had been apprenticed to Fenton, Murray & Wood of the 'Round Foundry' in Leeds and had latterly worked for Robert Stephenson & Co. Family tradition tells of a musically inclined young James being a chorister at Leeds Parish Church (now Leeds Minster) and actually building his own pipe organ at home. But instead of being an organ builder – and Leeds was home to several notable firms – Kitson turned to engineering. In this venture he was joined by Charles Todd (*c.* 1795–1852), who was also an alumnus of Fenton, Murray & Wood. The money came from David Laird, a prosperous Yeoman farmer. The works manager was John Chester Craven (1813–1887), who had also been apprenticed at the 'Round Foundry', and who would later come to prominence as locomotive superintendent of the London, Brighton & South Coast Railway. Fellow alumni from the 'Round Foundry' were David Joy (1825–1903), progenitor of the valve gear of the same name; Richard Peacock (1820–1889), one half of Beyer, Peacock & Co.; and the Krupps brothers.

James Kitson (1807–1885) partner in Todd, Kitson & Laird – the firm which built *Lion*. Kitson was a very prominent member of Leeds society.

The *Leeds Mercury* announced:

TODD, KITSON, and LAIRD, Engineers, BRASS & IRON FOUNDERS, RAILWAY FOUNDRY, HUNSLET LANE, LEEDS, Manufacturers of Locomotive Steam-Engines, Tenders, Carriage and Waggon Wheels, Axles, Springs, Stationary Steam Engines and Boilers, on the High and Low Pressure Principles, for Inclined Planes, Warehouses, Mills, &c. Also, Shafting and Gearing, Cranes, Turn-Tables, Pedestals or Chairs for Rails, Force and Lift Pumps, Cocks, Valves, Brass, Copper, and Iron Pipes, and Brass and Iron Castings of every Description.

TODD, KITSON and LAIRD beg leave to announce that they are now commencing the above Business in all its Branches, on the most improved Principles, and in entirely new Buildings erected for the Purpose; and trust that their Capabilities and assiduous Attention will enable them with regard to Facility, Punctuality and superior Workmanship, to give Satisfaction to all who may favour them with their Orders. Railway Foundry, Hunslet Lane, Leeds, Sept. 1st 1837. (*Leeds Mercury*, 2 September 1837)

Thus, the company had only been existence for a month when they received this lucrative contract from the L&M. It must have been an act of great faith on the part of Booth, and quite a gamble on the part of the Board of Directors, to order six locomotives from a newly established firm with no prior locomotive-building credentials. Sadly, the partnership was only short-lived, being dissolved in April 1839 almost as soon as the last engine for the L&M had been delivered. Todd joined forces with another Leeds engineer, John Shepherd Junior, as 'Shepherd & Todd', whilst Kitson formed a partnership with Laird as Kitson & Laird. This second partnership didn't last long either as in 1842 the firm of Kitson, Thompson & Hewitson was formed; William Watson Hewitson (*c.* 1814–1863) was a Newcastle Quaker who had been apprenticed to Robert Stephenson & Co. He later worked for Fenton, Murray & Jackson of Leeds in their locomotive shops, eventually becoming a draughtsman with Todd, Kitson & Laird.

James Kitson was one of the leading figures of Leeds. He was a Unitarian and attended Mill Hill Chapel in City Square and donated the lovely wrought-iron communion rail in 1847, and a memorial window was designed for his wife by William Morris in 1865. His youngest son, another James (1835–1911), became Lord Airedale. Kitson was Lord Mayor of Leeds in 1860 and 1861, a Justice of the Peace, Chairman of the Leeds Northern Railway and was the founding secretary and later President of the Leeds Mechanics' Institute – the handsome building of which by the Leeds architect Cuthbert Brodrick now houses Leeds City Museum. The minister at Mill Hill, Rev. Charles Wicksteed – part of the famous Wicksteed dynasty of engineers – was also a founding member and past president of the Mechanics' Institute. James Kitson was as an ardent liberal in politics, and a social reformer; the premises of Kitson & Laird were used to hold reform meetings in Leeds and also to host a dinner to honour John Bower, the Radical candidate for Hunslet in 1839. Kitson was also important in the founding of Hunslet Unitarian Church and School. His granddaughter, Jessie Beatrice Kitson (1876–1965), was the first female Lord Mayor of Leeds (1942–1943) and the fourth member of the family to hold the position.

This influx of orders from the L&M probably meant that Todd, Kitson & Laird were short-handed, as in July 1838 they were advertising via the *Leeds Times* for 'Two or Three Good Smiths' who were accustomed to 'locomotive work'; 'none but Steady, Sober, Work men need apply.'

Lion was the first locomotive to be delivered at a cost of £1,100 in Summer 1838. She had 5-foot-diameter coupled driving wheels and a pair of 3-foot 6-inch carrying wheels, cylinders 11 × 20 inches, and weighed in working order 14 tons 9 cwt 2 qr. James Kitson's obituary includes the tongue-in-cheek comment that part of the converted mill building in which their foundry was established had to be demolished so that Lion could be delivered. The *Leeds Times* of Saturday 4 August 1838 proudly announced:

James Kitson (1835–1911) enrobed as the First Baron Airedale and depicted in the great East Window of Mill Hill Chapel, Leeds, where the family were worshippers. (Rev. Jo James)

All that remains today of Kitson's Airedale Foundry, Leeds.

> Messrs. Todd, Kitson & Laird, of this town, have just completed their first locomotive engine manufactured for the Liverpool & Manchester Railway. The engine was exhibited to a number of respectable gentlemen on Tuesday last, who spoke in the most flattering terms of the excellence of its manufacture.

The *Leeds Mercury* of the same date added:

> New Loco-Motive Engine. We witnessed the trial on Monday last of a new and very powerful locomotive engine, built by Messrs. Todd, Kitson & Laird of this town, for the Manchester and Liverpool Railway. Benjamin Gott esq. and T. B. Pease esq., and several other gentlemen connected with railways in this neighbourhood, were present, and expressed, in the highest terms, their admiration the excellent workmanship and appearance of the engine.

Until *Elephant* and *Buffalo* had been delivered from Leeds, *Lion* and *Tiger* were temporarily employed as the banking or 'help up' engines on the Whiston and Sutton inclines, where one newspaper hoped that they would 'do the work of two engines'. *Lion*'s first driver was a Leeds lad called Joseph Greenall, who had probably been sent with her as a fitter from Todd, Kitson & Laird to help erect her on the opposite side of the Pennines. *Lion* and her sisters were probably despatched via the Leeds–Liverpool canal. *Lion*'s home shed was Manchester, whilst *Tiger* was based in Liverpool.

So impressed was Edward Woods (1814–1903), the chief engineer of the Liverpool & Manchester Railway from 1836–1845, with the standard of workmanship of *Lion* and

The family ties between *Lion* and the earlier *Planet* are apparent in this shot at the Science & Industry Museum. (David Boydell)

Tiger that they became the benchmark for all other locomotives to be delivered to the line. Indeed, written specifications for boilers issued by the Woods in October 1838 make reference to the high quality of the 'materials and workmanship' of the pair. Something of *Lion*'s original appearance on the Liverpool & Manchester can be gleaned from Wood's boiler specification. Boilers were of the 'long plate' variety, formed from four iron plates joined with longitudinal lap seams, rather than being formed of traditional 'barrels'. The boilers were specified to be 7 feet 6 inches long 'outside, between the smoke-box and the outside casing of the fire-box'. Francis Whishaw describes *Lion*'s boiler barrel, in November 1839, as being slightly shorter (7 feet 4 inches long), whilst Alexander Forsyth, the foreman of Ordsall Lane engine shed, notes 7 feet 5 inches. Woods specified boilers to be and 3 feet 3 inches in diameter but, because of the form of construction, it was actually slightly oval that of *Lion* being 3 feet 6 inches wide and 3 feet 3 inches high. The boiler was to be made of the 'best Low Moor plate' 5/8-inch thick and it was to be joined to the smokebox and firebox with angle irons and a double row of rivets. The smokebox was also Low Moor iron, 3/16-inch thick. The inner firebox was copper, 7/16 of an inch except that tube plate which was 5/8. There were 126 1 5/8-inch outside diameter brass tubes. The outer firebox was 3/8-inch Low Moor plate 'neatly and firmly riveted together, and the top must not rise above the top of the cylindrical boiler more than is necessary', suggesting that the firebox was more akin to that of *Planet* than the present boiler with its very high-crowned outer firebox. The boiler had two steam domes 14 inches diameter: one over the firebox, surmounted by a safety valve, and the second midway down the boiler barrel. A second safety valve was fitted on the boiler behind the chimney, and there was also a manhole 'fitted with a neat brass cap'.

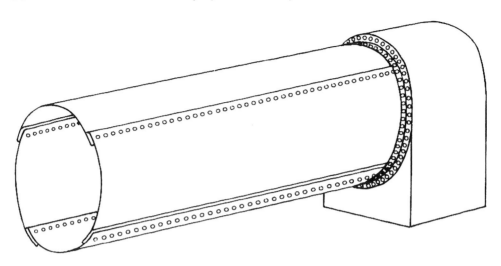

Construction of a 'long plate' boiler from four longitudinal plates rather than concentric 'barrels'. (Andrew S. Mason)

It was whilst employed as the banker on the Sutton and Whiston inclines that *Lion* was involved in the tragic explosion of *Patentee* on Monday 12 November 1838. *Patentee* was the pilot engine coupled to *Fury* (the train engine) at the head of a heavy train of forty-three loaded goods wagons (probably weighing 250 tons) assisted (Banked), from the rear, by the newly arrived *Lion*. Whilst toiling up the incline, Patentee blew up. The explosion, which was 'stated to have resembled the firing of a cannon, was heard at Prescot and other places, more than a mile distant'. According to the *Manchester Courier* (17 November 1838) 'The Engine was shattered to pieces, and the tubes were totally destroyed.' The engineman, Charles Warburton was found

> Forty yards distant … his right leg was broken, and his head terribly mangled … The Fireman … Samuel Jones, a lad of not more than eighteen years of age … was found in the opposite direction. His left leg was literally severed from his body, and lay two yards distant from it. (*Manchester Courier,* 17 November 1838)

After examining the wreck of *Patentee*, John Melling could not account for the explosion. The fusible plug had not blown, suggesting the water level had not dropped dangerously low; the boiler plates were found to have been sound; and he dismissed the idea that the crew had tampered with the safety valves as 'Warburton was an old and experienced engineer'. It is likely that the cause of the explosion was due to a fault inherent in the design of *Patentee* as the drag-pin (which connects the tender to the locomotive) was riveted directly to the back of the firebox, rather than to the frames, so when under extreme load, as *Patentee* was, the firebox could be literally ripped apart. Following the explosion, the Directors recommended that 'the staying of the Fire Box above the Fire Door and Boiler End next the Chimney were strong', suggesting the cause of the explosion lay not with the boiler but the firebox, and the drag-pin being riveted to it.

Lion was involved in a second accident in 1840 when she derailed, which was probably the result of a broken axle, which caused 'much damage to the machinery'. This accident probably explains *Lion*'s mismatched driving wheels: whilst the trailing pair have eighteen spokes, the leading wheels have only sixteen spokes, are of a different pattern, and were made by the firm of Rothwell & Co. of Bolton. It is unlikely that Todd, Kitson & Laird would have used wheels from Bolton, suggesting that these are in-service replacements. Liverpool Museums indicate they may have been second-hand from a Bolton & Leigh locomotive, which company used wheels of the same pattern and maker as the leading wheels on *Lion*. It should also be stated that the left- and right-hand crank axle horn guides are different. The left-hand horn guide has had its eight original mounting holes carefully filled and new ones drilled in slightly different locations. The right-hand horn guide is secured with ten bolts, suggesting it is a later replacement and that at some point in the locomotive's history the crank axle has been replaced.

With the delivery of the more powerful banking engines *Elephant* and *Buffalo* from Todd, Kitson & Laird in March 1839, *Lion* and *Tiger* were put on the more mundane duties of hauling goods trains. *Lion* is recorded in summer 1839 as regularly working 75-ton goods trains from Liverpool to Manchester and back, and being able to work them up the Whiston and Sutton inclines without any assistance. On a typical day, she was described as being in steam for over sixteen hours, but was in fact only doing seven hours of 'useful work' making four full trips from Manchester to Liverpool (120 miles in total), during which time she burned 12 cwt 1 qr 8 lb of coke, of which 2 cwt was going to waste keeping her in steam whilst she was standing idle. On average, she burned 39 lbs of coke per mile, or about half a pound of coke per ton per mile. Despite being in steam for such a long period, her driver and fireman were only paid per trip made rather than the number of hours spent with their engine.

Edward Woods records that of *Lion* and *Tiger*, *Tiger* was perhaps the better of the pair, generally using less coke and less water to move a heavier load than her sister. Either that, or *Tiger* had a more economical fireman!

An atmospheric period pairing of *Lion* and *Planet* at Liverpool Road Station, Manchester. (David Boydell)

Table 1: Performances of *Lion* and *Tiger*, Autumn/Winter 1839

Week Ending	Engine	Miles Run	Trips	Load	Weight	Coke/Trip	Coke/Mile
26.10.39	*Lion*	540	18	14	84 tons	13 cwt 14 lb	49.0 lb
	Tiger	420	14	13	78 tons	12 cwt 1 qr 18 lb	46.8 lb
16.11.1839	*Lion*	540	18	14	84 tons	13 cwt 2 qr 4 lb	50.5 lb
	Tiger	360	12	15	90 tons	12 cwt 1 qr 5 lb	45.9 lb
23.11.39	*Lion*	120	4	12	72 tons	14 cwt 1 qr 4 lb	53.7 lb
	Tiger	60	2	16	96 tons	11 cwt 1 qr	46.7 lb
30.11.39	*Lion*	180	6	11	66 tons	12 cwt 3 qr 19 lb	48.2 lb
	Tiger	420	14	15	90 tons	11 cwt 2 qr 22 lb	43.7 lb
7.12.39	*Lion*	360	12	13	78 tons	14 cwt 1 qr 25 lb	54.0 lb
14.12.39	*Lion*	360	12	12	72 tons	13 cwt 3 qr 12 lb	57.7 lb
21.12.39	*Lion*	120	4	11	66 tons	15 cwt 2 qr 14 lb	58.3 lb

Rebuild and Standardisation

In Autumn 1839 the L&M Directors empowered Henry Booth to reorganise the locomotive department. John Melling was given three months' notice to quit, and in his place John Dewrance (1803–1861) from Messrs Peel, Williams & Peel of Manchester was appointed as Locomotive Superintendent. All repair work was to be centralised at Edge Hill and some 10,000 square yards of land was purchased at Wavertree Lane in Liverpool to facilitate this. John Dewrance had an excellent working relationship with his chief Edward Woods, and together they carried out in-depth experiments on locomotive fuels, fuel and water consumption, valve gear and valves. They concluded that valves with short-travel and a limited amount of lap and lead did not promote fuel efficiency. Instead, Woods proposed the adoption of valves with longer travel (4 inches) and with lap and lead (1 inch). He also proposed to use a standard valve gear, that of William Barber Buddicom (1816–1887), which he developed at Edge Hill for the Grand Junction Railway around 1840/1841.

Upon his appointment, John Dewrance was faced with a rather motley collection of locomotives, including *Planet*, which dated from 1830. Woods' and Dewrance's locomotive policy was somewhat similar to that of the First Sea Lord Jackie Fisher at the turn of the twentieth century – 'scrap the lot'. Woods and Dewrance resolved to build new standard locomotives and, as a stopgap, to rebuild existing locomotives where possible. Adopting new valves was 'no easy task':

> On close examination it was discovered that, in many cases, there was no room in the steam chests for valves of greater lap; in others, that it was impossible to increase the length of travel. Therefore it was necessary to prepare, in the first instance, for the sacrifice of at least the cylinders, steam chests, working gear, and inside framing of several engines then needing repair, and eventually, as resources would permit, for replacing the Company's entire stock with new engines, all built according to one model. (Woods 1851: 13)

Dewrance reported to the Chairman on 16 December 1842 that locomotive construction had commenced at Edgehill and the locomotive fleet had been organised into three categories:

1. The "New" Engines are those which have been built entirely by the Company, and, which from the uniformity observed in their construction, rank *first* in value.

2. The "Rebuilt" Engines are such of the old Engines as have had all their parts renewed with the exception perhaps of the boiler, firebox and framing, and rank *second* in value.

3. The "Repaired" Engines are such of the old Engines have undergone thorough repair without altering the cylinders, gearing etc. to conform with the most approved models, and rank *third* in value. (Senate House Library, MS 584 (xix))

Lion and *Tiger* came under the second category, having been rebuilt at Edge Hill and 'turned out of the company's workshops' on 6 April and 14 May 1841. Examination of the locomotive reveals that the entire 'bottom end', other than the leading axle and wheels (see above), are of a piece and belong together; the crank axle, wheels, and valve gear all carry the same number, made with the same stamp. The frames too probably date from this rebuild. It is also likely that *Lion* was re-boilered at this time with a longer boiler, corresponding in length with the one carried in preservation. All in all, the rebuild of 1841 was pretty much creating a new locomotive in all but name and number. In fact some of these rebuilds cost over £850, compared to only £650 for one of Dewrance's new Bird class locomotives turned out from Edge Hill!

Edward Woods notes that between 1840 and 1842 some twenty-four new engines were built at Edge Hill and he 'broke up as many old ones', and that by December 1843 'every engine belonging to the Company has the improved valve' with 1-inch lap (25.4 mm), 4-inch (101.6 mm) travel and with wider steam ports. 'Great care' was taken in the casting of new cylinders to 'enlarge the area of the passage of exhaustion' to reduce back pressure in the cylinders as much as possible. *Lion*'s present valves have a travel of 3 13/16 inches (96.83 mm) and an outside lap of 13/16-inch (20.63 mm), so slightly less than Woods' specification, but probably acceptable in the early 1840s.

Buddicom's valve gear uses four fixed eccentrics to provide fore and back gear. The eccentric rods terminate in opposed V-shaped 'gabs', which can be raised or lowered from

Left: *Lion* was refitted with gab valve gear as developed by Buddicom at Edge Hill works. The gabs have opposed jaws which can be raised or lowered from pins on a rocking shaft. Here, forward gear is engaged. (Anthony Dawson/Museum of Liverpool)

Below: Buddicom's gab valve gear with which *Lion* is still fitted: A reversing lever; B reach-rod; C eccentrics; D back-gear eccentric rod; E fore-gear eccentric rod; F lifting links; G rocking-shaft; H valve-spindle. (Andrew S. Mason)

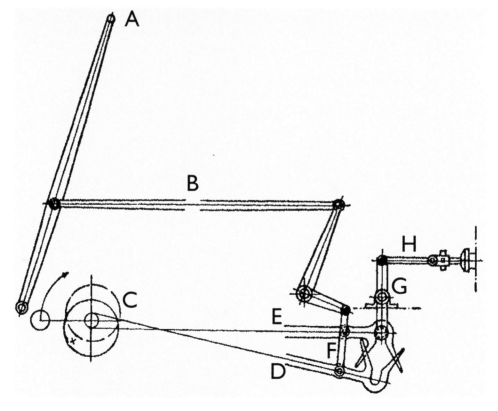

Lion's reversing lever. She is somewhat idiosyncratic to drive as to engage fore gear the reversing lever must first be unlocked and then pulled backwards! (Anthony Dawson/Museum of Liverpool)

the footplate by a single reversing lever. To engage fore gear, the lever is pulled backwards, lowering the downward-facing fore gear gabs onto pins on a rocking shaft. These in turn drive the valve spindles. Thus, to engage back gear, the reversing lever is moved forward. Because to engage fore gear the reversing lever is pulled backwards this set-up is known as 'left-handed' and because the valve spindles are not driven directly, as 'indirect' valve gear. *Lion* is also left-hand leading, which means that the left-hand crank is always ahead of the right hand.

Edward Woods and Dewrance both reported to the Gauge Commissioners in 1846 that they had standardised cylinder dimensions – 13 × 20 inches for 'luggage engines' and 12 × 18 inches for 'coaching engines' – and that there were no locomotives with differing cylinder sizes. Thus *Lion* (as a luggage engine), in theory, would have been rebuilt with 13 × 20 cylinders and thus have retained at least her crank axle. Dewrance, however, reported to the Board of Trade in 1845 that *Lion*'s cylinders were in fact 12 × 18 inches, the same as those used by 'coaching engines'. *Tiger* also carried 12 × 18 cylinders, whilst *Leopard*, *Panther*, *Elephant* and *Buffalo* all retained their original cylinder sizes. Thus, *Lion* probably received new cylinders in 1841 as part of the major rebuild. Given that the present valve gear and crank axle etc. all share the same stamps, this may argue for a stroke of 18 inches being adopted in 1841. Hence, no doubt, the differences evident in horn guides on the driving axle. Thus, the present cylinders (14 × 18 inches) may be those of 1841 re-bored, or, more likely, a replacement set of a larger bore but retaining the 18-inch stroke and valve travel, thus retaining the existing driving and valve gear geometry.

In rebuilt form, with new valves and valve gear, *Lion* was burning half the amount of coke per ton/mile: 24.9 lbs in December 1844 compared to 49.0 lbs of October 1839, suggesting that Woods was correct in his belief that longer travel valves with lap and lead would make better use of the steam, and thus increase fuel economy. There was no variable cut-off; *Lion* has a fixed cut-off of 81 per cent.

Driving Lion

Thanks to her gab valve gear, *Lion* is far easier to operate than *Planet* with her apparently bewildering array of shifting eccentrics, foot pedal and constantly wagging valve levers. There is only a single lever for fore and back gear. The regulator opens anti-clockwise (away from the driver) and is worked in and out via the helical quadrant, which means it is impossible to slam it shut in an emergency. Alan Middleton who drove *Lion* in Manchester in 1980 recounted:

> She was very docile, but a bit idiosyncratic. If you wanted to put her in forward gear, you had to pull the great heavy lever backwards … There was no breaks, so to slow her down you had to put her in reverse … She used very little coal, just a few rounds now and then. The problem was stopping her blowing off. It was never a problem to light up without a blower. It was run seven days a week and never got cold and so would always draw. She'd do anything you asked of her. She's smaller than *Furness 20* but had extra wheels under the cab. It'd run like the clappers on the straight and level but it took time to get there.

Cab view of *Lion*, taken at Crewe in 1988. The cab controls are very simple: boiler pressure gauge, whistle; regulator, water gauge and reversing lever. The regulator opens anti-clockwise, away from the driver.

Adrian Jarvis of Liverpool Museums adds:

> [Everyone] was delighted with the docility and smoothness of this ... Locomotive of 1838 vintage, together with a seeming ability to produce large amounts of steam from little or no coal ... *Lion* ... was faultless. The operation of *Lion*'s mechanical parts was faultless, and its brisk acceleration – and equally brisk retardation by the seemingly brutal method of engaging the opposite gear – soon dispelled any fears as to the difficulty of controlling the locomotive.

The only way to change gear is with the regulator closed, so there is no steam in the valve chest, but it was also quickly found that *Lion* does not like coasting to a halt in mid-gear, due to residual pressure in the cylinders and the accumulation of condensation. Having thus drifted to a halt, she could not be persuaded to change gear until the drain taps had been opened by hand from ground level, making a little whistle as they released pressure in the cylinders and any accumulated condensate. Thus, to slow down and reverse, the regulator was closed and the gear quickly changed, and as the engine drifted to a halt, steam reapplied (going through the steam circuit in the opposite direction) and used to create back pressure in the cylinders to slow down and eventually stop the locomotive. Skilled drivers could bring *Lion* to a stand and hold her stationary 'on the regulator'. This is a style of driving familiar to those who have worked with the replica *Rocket* and *Planet*.

One of *Lion*'s cast-brass oilers for reading oil into the cylinder, and also releasing condensate. (Anthony Dawson/Museum of Liverpool)

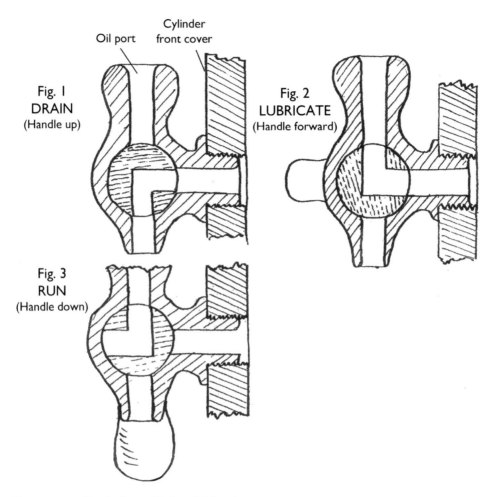

The operation of *Lion*'s oil pots. (Andrew S. Mason)

Later Career

The Liverpool & Manchester Railway amalgamated with the Grand Junction Railway in the summer of 1845. With the formation of the London & North Western Railway in 1846 *Lion* became No. 116 of the LNWR Northern Division, working on the Liverpool & Manchester Section. She continued to ply her trade with goods trains between Liverpool & Manchester for eleven years, until, in January 1857, *Lion* was transferred to the Stores Department on permanent way duties as Ballast Engine No. 14, stationed at Manchester. She probably lost her name at this time. Whilst working as a ballast engine one of her drivers was J. Waterworth, and fireman Thomas Baron. It was also during the 1850s that she was re-tyred at Crewe, and finally in May 1859 she was sold to the Mersey Docks & Harbour Board for £400. *Tiger*, her sister engine, was probably scrapped around 1850. The decision to dispose of *Lion*, and other obsolete locomotives, had been taken by John Ramsbottom (1814–1897), the recently appointed (1857) Locomotive Superintendent of the LNWR Northern Division, who was attempting to standardise motive power. Indeed, the decision to downgrade *Lion* to ballast duties in 1857 coincided with his appointment.

Lion looks at home posing on the Water Street Bridge, at Liverpool Road station, in February 2007. Manchester was *Lion's* 'home shed' whilst working on the Liverpool & Manchester Railway from 1838–1845. (David Boydell)

The Mersey Docks & Harbour Board had been in existence for only a year when they purchased *Lion*. Pressure from Parliament for Liverpool Corporation to divest itself of its docks interest via the Liverpool Docks Trustees resulted, in 1858, in the formation of the Docks & Harbour Board. The MD&HB also ran an extensive railway system, despite its early (1825) opposition to railways on the docks themselves. The Liverpool & Manchester Railway had a branch from its Wapping Goods station from the early 1830s, and a connection from the South Docks (MD&HB) to the LNWR at Wapping was in existence by 1851; it was extended, in 1853, from Wapping to Queen's Dock. Further branches and extensions were made from 1852–1860 and the system soon totalled 60 miles. This railway system was managed directly by the MD&HB and byelaws for the working of the railway were instituted in 1856. Under the MD&HB Consolidation Act (1858) the MD&HB were empowered to make 'reasonable charges' on outside users those who used the railways under their control.

The first locomotives owned by the MD&HB appear to have been a pair of second-hand locomotives, ordered at the request of the Dock Engineer in October 1858 to work the docks at Birkenhead. They were purchased from 'Messrs. Thompson & Co. at £500 including tenders'. Thompson & Co. were probably Thompson & Cole of the Hope Foundry, Bolton. They were Stephenson-type 0-4-2s with 14 × 18 inch cylinders, 5-foot driving wheels, and presumably gab valve gear, meaning that they share many similarities with *Lion* as she is today. As well as these two locomotives, the MD&HB also purchased workshop tools and equipment from Messrs Whitworth of Manchester, as well as sleepers, rails and spikes for Birkenhead Docks. In May 1859 the Dock Engineer recommended the purchase of additional motive power. The Works Committee recommended the purchase of three second-hand locomotives on 7 May 1859, which was approved by the Board five days later:

12 May 1859.
That the following offers of Locomotive Engines be, and they are hereby accepted, viz.-
From the London & North Western Railway Company, the Engine No. 14 for the sum of £400
From the Lancashire & Yorkshire Railway Company, of Engine No. 27 for the sum of £650
and of engine No. 25 for £550. (MP/9/2, Minute 12 May 1859)

The L&NWR approved the sale of 'Ballast Engine No. 14' to the MD&HB for £400 on 25 May 1859. *Lion* is not mentioned by name in the MD&HB minutes, and indeed the purchase of the locomotive in May 1859 is the only time it appears in the extensive (and detailed) MD&HB archive, and indeed the paper trail for *Lion* ends at this point. There is no archival evidence to link the locomotive purchased in 1859 with that discovered in 1923.

Thus, *Lion* was one of three locomotives purchased to work some element of the MD&HB system in Liverpool; the railway on the docks themselves were worked by horses until the 1870s. The fact that *Lion*'s carrying wheels – and we know they *are Lion*'s carrying wheels as they have the same stamps as the crank axle – were found with her in the pump house at Prince's Dock suggests that she was placed in the pump house as a complete, working locomotive (albeit minus tender), rather than having been used as a pump elsewhere. Therefore, it is likely that between 1859 and *c.* 1875 *Lion* was used as a locomotive by the MD&HB, and perhaps modified as a tank engine which would be far handier on the docks system.

The two former L&YR locomotives were No. 25 *Ouse* and No. 27 *Irk*. Both were delivered in January 1841. They were Stephenson-type 2-2-2 coaching engines with tall *arc-de-cloître* fireboxes. They had 95 psi boilers, 5-foot 6-inch driving wheels and 14 × 18 inch cylinders. *Irk*, built by William Fairbairn of Manchester, has the somewhat dubious history of having exploded on 30 January 1845 in Miles Platting Shed. *Irk* was in poor condition when she blew up at around 6 am on that fateful morning. She was thrown 20 yards across the shed, damaging another locomotive – *Trent* – and demolishing most of the roof. George Mills (driver), William Allcock (fireman) and William Stone (inspector) were killed and a deodand of £500 was placed on the engine. The safety valves had failed to open, the inquest finding that for the explosion to throw the engine through the shed roof, nearly 1,000 psi would have been needed! She was rebuilt in March 1845 and put back into service. Obsolete ten years later together with *Ouse*, *Irk* was at first offered for sale to the Demerara Sugar Co., before being sold to the MD&HB.

New Boiler

Whilst working for the MD&HB, *Lion* was re-boilered in 1865 at a cost of £300, the boiler being made in-house by the MD&HB. This is probably the boiler the locomotive still carries. However, when *Lion* was taking part in the filming of the *Titfield Thunderbolt* an ex-GWR fireman, who was in his seventies, recounted how his father had been involved in drilling, by hand with a ratchet drill, ninety or so holes in a boiler

Detail of *Lion*'s back-head, showing the brass plate carrying number '149'. Just visible is an inspection stamp. (Anthony Dawson/Museum of Liverpool)

tube plate for *Lion*, sometime around 1900. He also recalled that the boiler had been taken from another locomotive, No. 149, which number is still carried on the back-head of *Lion*'s boiler.

The boiler is of typical mid-nineteenth-century construction. It is formed from three rings of half-inch Low Moor iron that is lap riveted together, each ring consisting of two plates. The front and rear barrels have their joins running vertically along the centre line, whilst the middle barrel has its joints horizontally. The middle barrel overlaps the two end barrels.

The firebox has a raised 'waggon top' crown, similar to those 'Leeds type' boilers favoured by Manning Wardle or Hunslet. The raised firebox crown, surmounted by a pair of safety valves let into the manhole cover and the boiler barrel devoid of any fittings other than clack valves, is similar to that used on many mid-century saddle tank locomotives. It is thus possible that *Lion* was rebuilt at some stage in her career as an 0-4-2 saddle tank, which would be far more handy shunting on the Liverpool Docks than a tender engine. The boiler is substantially longer than the boiler recorded in 1839, being 8 feet 6 ½ inches long internally, with an internal diameter of 40 ½ inches. The outer firebox is just shy of 4 feet square and the copper inner firebox measures 39 ¾ inches × 40 ¾ inches. There are ninety-eight copper tubes, 2 inches outside diameter, 8 feet 6 inches long, a figure which corresponds with the specification for the 1865 boiler. The crown of the outer firebox is made from a single sheet of Low Moor iron, and the back plate is made from a single sheet, far larger than any which could have been produced in the 1830s or early 1840s. The size of the present boiler, and the very limited tolerances between the crank throws and the boiler cladding, and with the driving wheels running incredibly close to the smokebox suggest that it is a later replacement, and not original to the locomotive. However, it is over a foot longer than the boiler described by Whishaw in 1839, and if *Lion* were to maintain her present wheel size and wheelbase (12 feet overall at 6 feet centres) then the leading axle would pass through the cylinders! This again suggests the 1841 rebuilding created a virtually new locomotive. Whilst Edward Woods reports to the Gauge Commissioners, in 1846, that all boilers on the L&M were 9-foot long, this probably referred to the new-build Bird class, whilst the rebuilds perhaps had a bit more variation. There is a very high probability that the 1865 boiler embodies the main dimensions of that from April 1841.

The front tube plate is flat against the end of the boiler barrel attached via an angle iron flange ring outside the barrel. This ring is riveted to the boiler barrel through one flange of the angle, and through the other onto the tube plate itself. The tube plate itself is not a flat circular plate but has the form of an elongated 'D'. It extends downwards below the boiler barrel and has a slight kink to it to account for the inclination of the cylinders. Such a tube plate is shown in the Docks & Harbour Board specification, including the diameter of the cylinders being 14 inches. The tube plate is specified as being 4 feet 2 inches wide and 6 feet 7 inches from top to bottom, but no thickness is given.

The edge of the tube plate is turned over (by hand) to create a flange to which the plates of the smokebox are riveted. The smokebox itself is made up from four iron plates, riveted together using shaped angle irons. The front of the smokebox is bolted in place and is probably a replacement. It is likely the front plate was originally riveted in place. The smokebox doors, though similar to those found in 1923, are replacements made in 1930.

The boiler is joined to the firebox again using another flanging ring, which is riveted to the outside of the rearmost barrel of the boiler and slightly wraps around the vertical section of the outer firebox. The regulator is of the 'Crewe type', which further dates the present boiler to the 1840s or later. There is no evidence of the drawbar ever being riveted to the firebox back-head in typical nineteenth-century manner, suggesting it was either carried on the frame (if a tender engine), or perhaps reinforcing the theory that *Lion*, at the latter stage of her career as an MD&HB locomotive, was a tank engine. The boiler carries the inspecting marks of the Manchester Steam Users' Association, a regulatory body for the inspection and insurance of stationary steam boilers, established in Manchester by William Fairbairn in 1854. For many years, boiler inspection was voluntary, until the law was changed in 1901 making it compulsory. The boiler was repaired in June 1902 and inspected by the MSUA to a pressure of 70 psi. This was evidenced by a stamp on the back-head: 'REP.D TEST 70LB 20.06.02 W.E. M.S.U.A.' Stamps of a similar font reading 'LOW MOOR' can be found elsewhere on the outer firebox.

Dock Duty

After working for over a decade on the railway system of the MD&HB, *Lion* was retired *c.* 1874 and put to work driving the chain pump that drained the Prince's Graving Dock facility, which came into use in January 1875. The traditional version of events, that *Lion* was purchased in 1859 for immediate use as a pump engine in Prince's Graving Dock, is therefore not correct. Furthermore, that *Lion*'s trailing axle

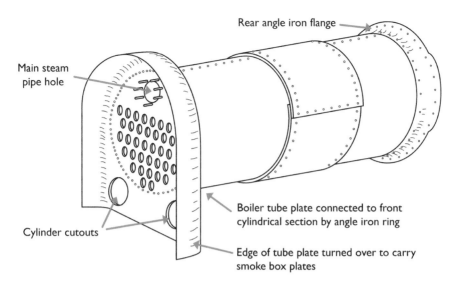

Main steam
pipe hole

Rear angle iron flange

Boiler tube plate connected to front
cylindrical section by angle iron ring

Edge of tube plate turned over to carry
smoke box plates

Cylinder cutouts

Lion's present boiler is made from three wrought-iron barrels lap riveted together and joined to the smokebox and firebox with a continuous flange ring. The tube plate is a single D-shaped sheet of iron drilled to take the boiler tubes as well as the cylinders. It is turned over around its outer edge to take rivets for the smokebox. (Andrew S. Mason)

Above left: Detail of the join between the boiler barrel and smokebox: the tube plate lays flat against the end of the barrel and is joined to it with the flange ring. The edge of the tube plate is turned over to form a flange onto which smokebox plates are riveted. (OLCO)

Above right: Detail of the joint between the boiler and outer firebox. The outer firebox is made from five sheets of iron. All the rivets are hand-closed. (OLCO)

Lion's boiler was repaired and inspected in 1902 by the Manchester Steam Users' Association, as recorded by this stamp on the firebox back-head. (OLCO)

and wheelset was found dumped in the pump house suggests that *Lion* was taken there as a complete, working locomotive and those parts, which were removed during the alterations so that she worked the pump gear, were simply abandoned where she was. Once *Lion* was installed in the pump house it was probably too much effort to recover the wheelset, and they languished in the pump house to be rescued along with the engine. Thus, it is likely that between 1859 and *c.* 1874 *Lion* was in fact a working locomotive on the MD&HB system and had not been previously cannibalised to work a pump elsewhere.

The Prince's Dock is the most southerly of the Liverpool docks. William Jessop and John Rennie prepared the plans for the dock – construction of which commenced in 1810 by William Foster – and it opened on 19 July 1821 (although unfinished), the day of the Prince Regent's coronation as George IV. During the construction it was alleged that Foster had purchased more stone than was needed and once this scandal broke, he quickly resigned. Liverpool Riverside Station (opened in 1895) was situated between the dock and the Mersey.

The Prince's Graving Dock facility, i.e. a dry dock, was built at the south end of the Prince's Dock between 1872 and 1874, and the graving dock itself was formed from a redundant link between the Prince's and George's Docks. The Dock Committee of the MD&HB records on 22 January 1875 that 'the Graving Dock at the South End of Prince's Dock is now complete and ready for use'. Thus, the date of *Lion* coming into use to work the pumps with which the dock was drained was in late January 1875. The dock and its pump house were demolished in the 1990s. The pump house was an elegant Italianate structure of four bays with a hipped roof topped with a louvred ventilator. The front facade had brick pilasters and a moulded cornice. The proposed chimney to carry away smoke from a more conventional pumping engine was never built.

In order for *Lion* to work as a pump, her carrying wheels were removed together with half of the carrying wheel horn guides. Her coupling rods were removed, and a gear wheel attached to her right-hand-driven axle, which, via a gear train and bevel gears, worked the chain pump mechanism. Her leading wheels were fixed in a cradle and as the pump was only unidirectional it was 'unnecessary to reverse the gab motion, except when a mishap occurs to the pump buckets, and that is not often'. The chain pump was incredibly crude:

> Consisting of boards, spaced by chains, running over pulleys top and bottom, like an endless moving ladder. These boards moved up a vertical channel, with small clearance, brining up a little water on each board from a sump from the dock beneath. (*The Locomotive*, March 1932)

Although the pump was unidirectional, *Lion*'s valve gear was kept in working order so that the pumps could be reversed in case of a mishap. The chain pump was crude but effective, and apparently one well-suited to the turgid waters of the Mersey. *Lion* was clearly at work by 1880, as in that year the MD&HB purchased 150 tons of coke for the pump engine at Prince's Graving Dock, and similar amounts are noted in MD&HB accounts for tenders for the supply of coal and coke later in the century.

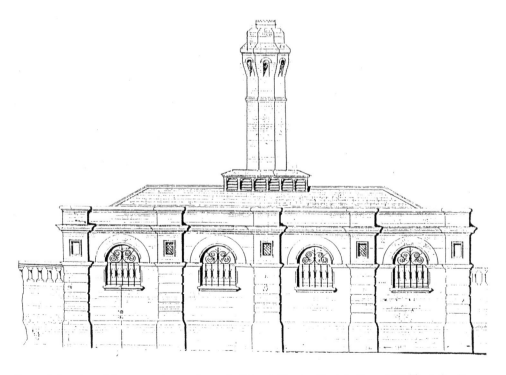

External elevation of the proposed pump house for Prince's Graving Dock facility, *c.* 1875. The lofty chimney was never built. Sadly, the pump house was demolished in the 1990s. (OLCO)

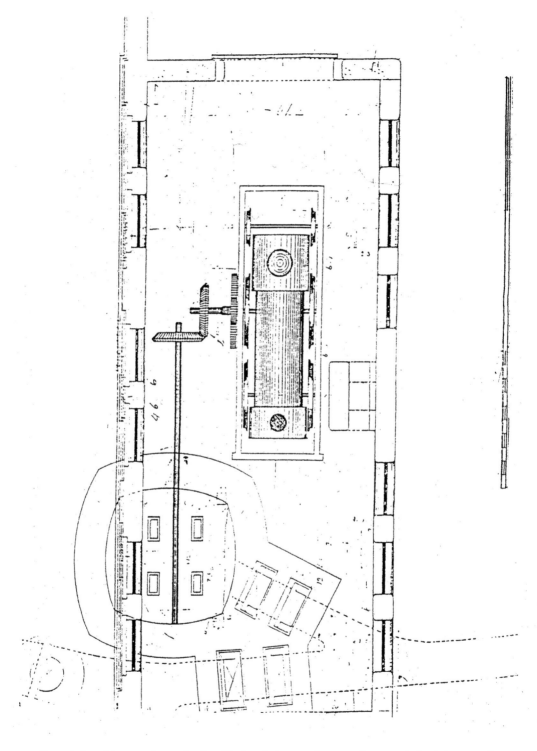

Ground plan of the pump house showing *Lion* installed as a stationary engine to work the chain pump. A gear train and bevel gearing on the driven axle provided power for the chain pump. (OLCO)

Chapter 2

Rescue and Restoration

Lion as she was in 1923, still working the chain pump in Prince's Graving Dock. Steam was supplied by an external 'donkey boiler' fed directly to the steam chests. Of note, the long copper blast pipe extends into the base of the chimney. (OLCO)

Lion spent over fifty years working as a pump at Prince's Dock, where she was first discovered in 1919, when the attention of the MD&HB Works Committee was drawn to the presence of the veteran locomotive in June of that year. But nothing was done about preserving the locomotive. Then, in January 1923 *The Locomotive Magazine* described how

> Within a few yards of the busy landing-stage at Liverpool and still doing duty as a stationary engine for working the pumps at the graving dock, Prince's Dock, is an interesting old locomotive that certainly dates back to the 'forties' ... and has been employed on its present duty for the past thirty-five years. (*The Locomotive*, 15 January 1923)

Steam was, by then, supplied via an external boiler and piped into the pump house as *Lion's* boiler was in poor condition. The working of the gab valve gear was demonstrated to a reporter from *The Locomotive* by a member of MD&HB staff. A photograph was included along with the details that the old locomotive, according to 'one of the old servants of the Harbour Board', had originally carried the name *Lion* and that it had belonged to the LNWR. *The Locomotive Magazine* suggested it had probably belonged to the Manchester & Birmingham Railway (one of the constituents of the LNWR) and that the dimensions of the locomotive corresponded with M&B No. 12 and No. 13, both of which were disposed of in 1874 and 1875. *Lion* is clearly neither of those two locomotives as they were both 2-2-2s built by William Fairbairn of Manchester. *The Engineer* picked up the story, so too the *Liverpool Echo*. This does bring a bit of a problem with the positive identification of *Lion*: nowhere in the LNWR or MD&HB minutes regarding the sale and subsequent purchase of Ballast Engine No. 14 is *Lion* actually named and, indeed, the purchase of the locomotive by the MD&HB is the only time Ballast Engine No. 14 appears in MD&HB minutes. Whilst oral tradition passed down via MD&HB staff suggest *Lion* is in fact *Lion*, there is no paper trail. And, of course, the memory can be fallible. Thus there is nothing to link the locomotive found in 1923 with that sold by the LNWR in 1859, and no evidence to suggest whether it was Ballast Engine No. 14 that ended its days working the pump in Prince's Graving Dock, or another locomotive hitherto unknown.

It is possible to rule out both of the ex-LYR locomotives purchased at the same time as *Lion* as they were both 2-2-2s, although their boiler and cylinder dimensions and type of valve gear correspond with the preserved *Lion*. The two 0-4-2s purchased from Thompson Cole, however, could be candidates. The first positive identification of the pump house engine as *Lion* was by E. L. Ahrons in November 1923, who also ascribed the builder Todd, Kitson & Laird – although there was no builders' plate on the engine, and the current plate is a twentieth-century copy. Thus, the identification of *Lion* is based upon oral tradition alone.

Although the existence of *Lion* was now recognised, once again no one thought of rescuing her and presenting her to a museum. Things were to change a few years later. In 1925 the Stockton & Darlington Railway had celebrated its centenary, which included a cavalcade of early locomotives, and, conscious that the centenary of the Liverpool & Manchester Railway was fast approaching, members of the Liverpool Engineering Society began to look towards the rescue and restoration of *Lion*. In order to do so they formed the Old Locomotive Committee. It is not certain when the first meeting was held – the oldest surviving minutes are dated 21 October 1927, but there is nothing in these minutes to suggest it was the first meeting. Membership included Sterry B. Freeman who was also

Another view of *Lion* in her pump days; the boiler is devoid of any cladding. Note the water tank mounted above the boiler. Of note is the timber staging built around the rear of the engine for firing and 'driving' purposes. (OLCO)

chairman of the Liverpool Engineering Society. He was the engineering superintendent of the 'Ocean Steamship Company', and 'had the ear' of Richard Holt, who was not only a director of the Ocean Steamship Co. but also chairman of the Mersey Docks & Harbour Board. On 27 June 1927 Freeman wrote to Lieutenant-Commander William Fletcher, one of the leading figures in the preservation of *Lion*:

> Mr Richard Holt has brought up the matter with the engineer [Mr Newell] at the Dock Board, who tells him the engine is doing very useful work and cannot be dispensed with without remodelling the pumping arrangements at the dock at a considerable expense … I have asked Mr Holt to pursue the matter further and we may hear more at a later date.

Fletcher, a member of the Liverpool Engineering Society, appears to have been the driving force behind the rescue of *Lion*: he 'became such a damn nuisance that, largely for the sake of peace [we] accepted his proposal that we should save *Lion*'.

The Liverpool Engineering Society formed the 'Old Locomotive Committee' (OLCO) for the rescue and preservation of *Lion*. The committee consisted of: Professor G. E. Scholes, of Liverpool University; T. R. Wilton Consultant and Emeritus Professor, Liverpool University; Lt-Cdr. W. M. Fletcher, consultant marine engineer; W. H. McMenemey; John Dykes, principal surveyor for Lloyds registry; F. Gaskin, deputy water engineer, Liverpool; B. Rathmell, a refrigeration consultant.

How *Lion* appeared when first recovered from the pump house: devoid of any boiler cladding; lacking fly-cranks and coupling rods and shorn of her trailing wheels. Boiler fittings such as the sight-glass and the regulator quadrant have been removed prior to transport to Crewe for restoration. (OLCO)

Newell, the Harbour Board engineer, attended a meeting of the committee on 12 December 1927, and following this meeting Fletcher was able to write to George Woolliscroft of the LMS that the dock engineer was 'taking a [more] sympathetic interest' in the rescue of *Lion* and was taking it to the next Board meeting, held on 16 December 1927:

> The feeling of the Committee was that the Old Locomotive at the Prince's Graving Dock should be handed over to the Liverpool Engineering Society, and it was decided to invite tenders for the necessary new plant.

A steam-driven chain pump would have been quite an anachronism, especially since the Prince's Graving Dock had been closed for several months, from November 1925, for modernisation and alterations which led to it being completely drained. Thereafter matters moved swiftly. An electric pump was ordered to be purchased in January 1928 and in February it was reported in the Docks and Harbour Board minutes that the cost of a new electric pump would be £1,728 4s 6d, which, on 2 March 1928, was ordered to be installed. *Lion* remained in her pump house until 17 September 1928, and her removal was featured in the local and national press, including a photograph in *The Illustrated London News* (29 September 1928).

Throughout this period OLCO had been in contact with both the LMS at Derby and Crewe, and with Colonel Edwin Kitson Clark (1866–1943), a grandson of James Kitson and chairman of Kitson & Co., Leeds. Whilst he was supportive of the restoration of the locomotive, given the financial difficulties his firm was then in (the receivers were called in 1934 and the firm wound up in 1938) he could not restore *Lion* at little or no cost. The LMS, conscious of the PR coup of the LNER in 1925, were more amenable to the suggestion. An initial quote for £110 to 'recondition … the *Lion* engine' was issued by the LMS and fundraising by OLCO began in earnest and by February 1929 'the amount raised comfortably exceeded the sum of £110'. The estimate of £110 did not include the cost of transport to Crewe, or the cost of any boiler repairs or springs. Happily for all concerned, on 16 March 1929 Sir Henry Fowler, the Chief Mechanical Engineer of the LMS wrote:

> It is the intention of the Company [LMS] to forgo the usual overhead charges which are included in the figure of £110, so that the actual charge for reconditioning the engine itself should be much less than £100.

In other words, Crewe Works had been given *carte blanche* to restore *Lion*, the final cost (which included building the tender) being nearly twice the initial quote!

A front three-quarter view of *Lion* showing how intact the locomotive was when recovered. The height of the firebox crown is very apparent in this view. The 'core' of the locomotive remains essentially the same to this day. (OLCO)

Restored at Crewe

In order to restore *Lion* to something close to an early nineteenth-century appearance advice was sought from J. G. H. Warren, who had originally been in the drawing office of Robert Stephenson & Co., and who in 1923 had published a monumental centenary history of that firm; A. E. Forward of the Science Museum; and Colonel Kitson Clark. It was decided to 'restore' the locomotive to a supposed 1840s appearance.

A committee to oversee the restoration of *Lion* was formed at Crewe works, chaired by Sir Henry Fowler. Committee members included: H. P. M. Beames, who had been CME to the LNWR 1920–1922, and latterly Mechanical Engineer at Crewe; W. M. Fletcher of OLCO; J. G. H. Warren, historian; G. W. Woolliscroft OBE M. I. Mech. E., of the LMS.

This group met in October 1929. The old chimney was too rotten so a new chimney, measuring 13 feet from the rail head, was to be provided. It was similar to the one shown for the L&M Dewrance locomotive *Ostrich* in E. L. Ahron's book detailing the history of British locomotives 1825–1925. Oral tradition suggests an old LNWR chimney was found and used but this is unlikely. All the old boiler fittings – gauge glass, clack valves, wash-out plugs etc. – were to be replaced with new. Warren was to prepare drawings for the leather-covered buffers (costing £10), as well as springs for the wheels; originally it was thought the locomotive (somewhat unlikely) had no springs! Vacant bolt holes on the inner frames indicated where previous spring-hangers were attached for the inner set of crank-axle bearings. Wheel splashers, footplates and handrails were made from new, again with reference to *Ostrich*, and there is evidence of electric welding on these components. New smokebox doors were made from drawings produced by Warren. Warren also

This drawing of *Ostrich*, a member of John Dewrance's Bird class of locomotives, was used as the inspiration behind much of the 1929–1930 restoration of *Lion*.

proposed fitting a copper 'firebox shell' to replicate an 1840s *arc-de-cloître* firebox, which is considered today a distinguishing feature of *Lion*, despite it being a piece of 1930s artifice. In the matter of the firebox casing, Warren sought the advice of E. A. Forward at the Science Museum who agreed with the fitting of the copper casing. Colonel Kitson Clark, however, was opposed to such a move:

> The firm [Kitsons] did not like brass domes and covers not only because they dazzled the engine crew but because they were expensive to the customer.

He also added that such embellishments were 'vulgar'. This firebox cover cost £15 and was made by a coppersmith at Crewe named Williams, who eventually became chief foreman of the Crewe coppersmith's shop, and later a senior trades union president. The firebox cover radically altered *Lion*'s appearance; although familiar to generations of railway enthusiasts it is not authentic.

Whilst there is no reference to the locomotive being either re-tubed or having its cylinders re-bored, both are likely to have taken place. Although stated to be 14 inches bore, *Lion*'s cylinders are in fact 14 1/8 inches. Copper ferrules found in the firebox tube plate in 1979, to accommodate new tubes in a worn tube plate, are probably evidence of re-tubing at Crewe. The ferrules were a cost-effective means of reducing worn tube holes in the copper tube plate without having to carry out expensive firebox repairs. A new wash-out plug in the smokebox tube plate was provided, so too a mechanical lubricator, which was tucked away in a most inconvenient position behind the leading left-hand-side splasher to provide lubrication to the cylinders.

The drag-pin bolted directly to the rearmost timber transom, which was not designed to be load bearing. It's no wonder that the drag-pin and transom worked loose and had to be replaced several times in preservation. (OLCO)

It was also noted that the wheel tyres were worn, and in the case of the right-hand leading wheel the tyre was in fact loose and needed shimming up, but given that the engine was not expected to be at work after it had completed running circles at Wavertree Recreation Ground, this and many other small tasks were overlooked. Also new were the outside cranks and coupling rods. The boiler was insulated and clad with mahogany strips. The nameplates are also products of Crewe Works.

Whilst in use as a pumping engine, part of the trailing wheel horn guides had been cut off, presumably to release the wheelset. These damaged horn guides were skilfully welded

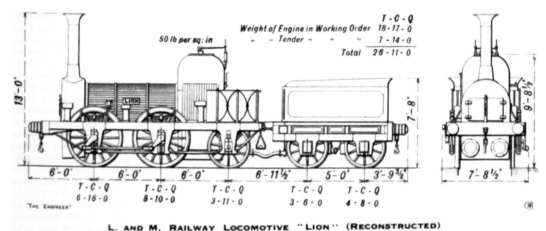

General arrangement drawing of *Lion* produced by the LMS at Crewe Works in 1929.

Lion as she appeared fresh from overhaul in 1930: the wheels, tender tank and cab railings were painted LNWR dark green; the smokebox was black and the frames (locomotive and tender) 'red-brown'.

up at Crewe. Luckily, the original trailing wheels had been left dumped in the pump house and could be recovered and reused. Again, perhaps because of the limited life expectancy of *Lion*, the transom joining the frames behind the firebox was replaced with a simple timber beam to which the drag-pin, which carried the drawbar linking the engine and tender, was secured. Putting the drag-pin on a relatively flimsy piece of timber transferred load stresses from the boiler to the main frame (which was not designed for such a task) and, furthermore, this timber cross-beam has had to be replaced on several subsequent occasions having failed in service.

The Tender

One final controversial aspect of the restoration is the tender. In his 1930 exhibition notes, Warren states that it was 'modified' from a former Furness Railway tender, whilst *The Engineer* (14 November 1930) records that 'the four-wheeled tender has been adapted from an early tender from the Furness Railway, and is very similar to those in use about 1840'. Adrian Jarvis notes (1987), 'As there was no tender, Crewe cut down one attached to an old Furness Railway engine at the works for scrapping.' A drawing was supplied by Robert Stephenson & Co. as the basis of the new tender.

The tender is in fact cannibalised from three former FR tenders utilising the wheelsets, axle boxes, horn guides, and tank. The brake gear came from an FR locomotive. The leading wheelset (axle No. 2949) came from Furness Railway No. 118 built by Sharp, Stewart in 1881 and scrapped at Crewe in 1927. The trailing wheelset (axle No. 2278) from FR No. 25 was built in 1873 and scrapped in 1916, but the tender obviously kept in service behind another locomotive. The underkeeps for both wheelsets derive from FR No. 26 of 1873 which was scrapped in 1930. Both wheelsets were re-tyred by Vickers of Barrow in 1900. No identifying numbers could be found on the tender tank, so its origins remain unknown. Of course, wheelsets can be changed, and these parts could have come from only a single vehicle. Although once thought to be 'fitted with 4-wheel tender of 12066 of FR, 1865', the stamped numbers on the tender components rule that out. *Lion*'s tender definitely originates with the Crewe restoration.

The cost of the 'tender overhaul' by the LMS was £60, one of the more expensive items of the restoration. The Model Engineer LBSC 'Curly Lawrence' was very dismissive of it:

> I've come to the conclusion that the merchant who built it must have been short of material, and lacking in bawbees as well. Apparently he went on the scrounge among the railway yards, found a few old sleepers. some bits of metal, and a discarded water cistern. Using a couple of the sleepers, he chawed out a pair of ragtime frames, and assembled them with a sleeper at each end. Then he found he that his water cistern was too low, so he copped up another sleeper, and put the bits between the cistern and the frame, to bring it level with the footplate. Unofficial history doesn't tell us where he got the wheels, but he must have gone down the coal-merchant's siding and snaffled the brake gear off a Moger or a Stephenson Clarke. To make a space for coal, he got a hammer and chisel, and chopped a slit halfway along each side of the top of the cistern, bending the bit down until it touched the bottom, and soldering up all the seams. Of course, I may be wrong, but that's what the whole business looks like.

During cosmetic restoration at Liverpool Museums (2008) it was found that the tender horn guides and wheels still carry FR Indian red paint. The horn guides have clearly been

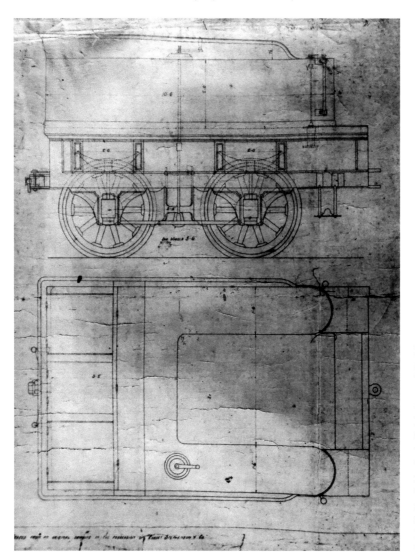

Drawings
supplied
by Robert
Stephenson &
Co. of
Darlington
for the new
tender to run
with *Lion*. The
finished product
used parts
reclaimed from
former Furness
Railway tenders.
(OLCO)

modified and drilled to receive new mounting bolts. The tender wheels and axles are far more robust than the carrying wheels of the engine, and were clearly intended to carry a much larger, heavier vehicle: typical Sharp, Stewart tenders of the 1870s had a 9-foot 6-inch wheelbase and weighed around 21–22 tons, when the present tender weighs 7 tons 14 cwt with a 5-foot wheelbase.

The tender tank has been shortened at the front; the back plate is heavily pitted and during the cosmetic restoration at Liverpool the conservator found corrosion where the typical Sharp, Stewart tender toolbox would have sat against the back of the tank. The tank is made in typical mid-nineteenth-century manner, with plates riveted to angle irons, but there is also evidence of 1930s welding. The underframe is made from soft wood, and clearly not intended for a long service life.

To sum up, the appearance of *Lion* – particularly the firebox cover and tender – are products of the 1930s restoration, and not representative of how *Lion* would have looked during her operational life on the Liverpool & Manchester Railway or LNWR.

Side view of the 1930-built tender behind *Lion*. The frames are made from soft wood; the tank, wheels, axles and axle boxes are recycled from three former Furness Railway tenders. (Anthony Dawson/Museum of Liverpool)

Rear view of the tender; the sidechains are a product of the 1979 restoration. (Anthony Dawson/ Museum of Liverpool)

Standing on *Lion*'s footplate and looking back into the coal space. The water filler is prominent, so too is the hand brake, air brake valve and air brake pressure gauge. (Anthony Dawson/ Museum of Liverpool)

The Railway Centenary

It is not known when *Lion* first steamed in preservation, but members of the OLCO had a ride on her in steam at Crewe on 11 July 1930. A second visit was made by them ten days later when there was still a considerable amount of work to do. It was reported by the national and local press that *Lion* was transferred from Crewe to Liverpool during late February 1930.

As part of the celebrations to make the centenary of the Liverpool & Manchester Railway in September 1930, *Lion* ran around a circular track at Wavertree Recreation Ground with a train of six specially constructed replica carriages; three first class and three standing-only third class (although the Liverpool & Manchester Railway didn't run such crude vehicles). The fare was 1s for first class and 6d third class. The first train headed by *Lion* was fittingly driven by Colonel Kitson Clark. One newspaper reported:

> Yorkshire visitors will find special interest in the Lion. It was built at Leeds in 1838, by Todd, Kitson & Laird, for the Liverpool & Manchester Railway, and was probably the first locomotive built by that firm (*Derbyshire Advertiser*, 19 September 1930.)

She was joined at Liverpool by replicas of *Rocket* and *North Star*, together with *Columbine* and *Cornwall*. The opportunity was also taken to pose her alongside the LNER's most up-to-date locomotive, the W1 'Hush Hush' No. 10000. A non-operable replica of *Northumbrian*, together with a replica of the Duke of Wellington's coach, was also built as part of the Railway Pageant. Sadly, these replicas were subsequently broken up.

It was generally believed in 1930 that, following her final fling with the 'Old Time Train', *Lion* would be allowed an honourable retirement, with a place of honour on a plinth over the buffer-stops between platforms 3 and 4 at Lime Street station. By a lease signed on 1 October 1930, the Liverpool Engineering Society had the right to keep *Lion* there for a peppercorn rent for a period of 999 years. *Lion* went on display, after much hand-shaking and suitable speeches, on 15 September 1931, the 101st anniversary of the Liverpool & Manchester Railway.

Lion as she appeared with her train of six replica coaches for the Railway Centenary, which she hauled around a circular track at Wavertree Recreation Ground in September 1930. (Museum of Liverpool)

Lion in steam in Liverpool with members of the Old Locomotive Committee. From left to right: Messrs McMenemy, Rathmell, Scholes, Fletcher, Dykes, Gaskin, and Wilton. (Museum of Liverpool)

As part of the Railway Centenary celebrations, *Lion* was on display with the LNWR replica *Rocket*; the GWR replica of *North Star*; LNWR *Columbine* (then erroneously thought to be the first locomotive built at Crewe) and *Derwent* from the Stockton & Darlington Railway.

Chapter 3

A Film Star

Two Centenaries and a Queen

Lion's retirement at Lime Street lasted only a few years. In April 1937 *Lion* was taken down from her resting place for her first film role, appearing in *Victoria the Great* starring Anna Neagle, as Victoria, and Anton Walbrook, as Albert. *Lion* was transported to Crewe for overhaul, which the railway correspondent of the *Derby Daily Telegraph* noted, 'A certain amount of work, I gather, will have to be carried out to make it possible to run this engine again if the experts' report suggests the work be only of a comparatively minor nature.' On the back of this report, *Lion* and her six coaches (then in store at Derby) would be loaned to the film company. The railway scenes – notably Victoria's first railway journey – were filmed on a siding at Bricket Wood on the Watford St Albans (Abbey) Line where *Lion* performed well, albeit for one exception. Whilst standing idle she was prone to blowing-off violently from her safety valves, often resulting in scenes being suspended, especially those involving dialogue. Her crew for the occasion were driver Johnson and fireman Males, both from Watford shed, who were apprehensive about 'the thing' (as they referred to *Lion*) not blowing up! The demands of filming led to frustration amongst the crew:

Lion takes centre stage during the filming of *Victoria the Great* at Bricket Wood in April 1937. (OLCO)

'Steam up in five minutes' would come the request; Fireman Males would stoke as if his life depended on it and cover the crinolined extras with an unwelcome black smoke. At the end of five minutes they proudly announced that they had raised steam, they were likely to be told 'not for half an hour yet' and so they would have to run down the line away from the sensitive 'mikes' to let *Lion* 'blow off' for five or ten minutes. (*Railway Magazine*, August 1937)

Other short trips were necessary to work the pumps to put water back into the boiler. *Lion* was then the oldest working locomotive in Britain, and the *Yorkshire Post* (15 June 1837) left its readers in no doubt as to her Leeds origins. Colonel Kiston Clark remarked *Lion* was the first of six locomotives built by his firm for the Liverpool & Manchester Railway and the first to leave the Airedale foundry. He noted that *Lion* was 'the oldest locomotive in the world that will go by steam power' and told the *Yorkshire Evening Post* he thought 'the frames, cylinders, valves and driving gear are the originals' but 'the boiler is later in date, and the raised firebox crown is not original'. *Lion* was then the only locomotive 'which has the original gab valve motion' in service in the country.

The film opened at Leicester Square on 17 September 1937, and *Lion*'s involvement made her a celebrity in the city of her birthplace. The *Yorkshire Post* reported:

Victoria and the Lion … Among various the lesser incidents in the Queen's life will be shown her first journey by train. In the film this train is drawn by the now-famous *Lion* the Hunslet-built locomotive which has just completed a hundred years of active life. Its birthplace was a tiny shed in Hunslet – so small that the side had to be taken down before the engine could be removed – and its builder was James Kitson who, in 1837, had just started the Airedale foundry. The *Lion* was the first of 5,000 locomotives which were to be turned out by this firm in the next hundred years.

Fresh from filming *Victoria the Great*, *Lion* and her six coaches travelled to the North Wales coast to be used in an official LMS film, filmed on the line from Llandudno Junction to Colwyn Bay. J. M. Dunn, who was Foreman Fitter at Llandudno from 1935–1939, described the preparations that were made:

The old Liverpool and Manchester Railway engine *Lion* and a train of replica contemporary coaches having been recently engaged in the making of the film on the life of Queen Victoria, 'Sixty Glorious Years', it was decided that a cinematograph film should be made of *Lion* and its train of 1835, the Coronation and its train of 1911 and the 'streamlined' (or tinned – as I prefer to call it) Coronation and its train of 1937. To this end arrangements were made for the respective engines and trains to run specially for the purpose over the main-line between Llandudno Junction and Colwyn Bay.

Lion and her train arrived on the night of Thursday, the 10th June 1937 from Bricket Wood on the St Albans branch where they had been previously performing. They were all loaded up on crocodile trucks and ran as a special train, the Crewe 36-ton crane coming down to unload them in the morning. On Saturday, the 12th June we had *Lion* in steam and ran some trial trips about the yard when she acquitted herself well. Later in the day the other two trains arrived and at 5.30 on the morning of Sunday the 13th June I went to the shed in readiness for the event.

Standing on-shed at Llandudno, 11 June 1937, looking diminutive compared to more modern motive power. (L&NWR Society)

All four lines between Colwyn Bay and Llandudno Junction were closed for filming purposes between 7.30 am and 9.30 am so that all three trains, accompanied by the fourth press and film camera train, could run parallel to each other:

> There had been a thunderstorm over night and the light was very bad ... The trains travelled, each slightly in advance of the other, on adjacent lines and the journey was made without mishap. It was thought that *Lion* would be unable to propel her train back to Llandudno Junction in 'back gear' so an engine was sent to pull the old train back but this precaution proved to be unnecessary as *Lion*, like the two Coronations easily shoved her train back to the starting place, a distance of 4 miles. It was a wonderful occasion as *Lion* was the oldest workable steam locomotive in the world and it was a great privilege to be associated with and present at a run of such a historic machine under its own steam. The old engine ran wonderfully well but was of necessity 'light' at the safety valves owing to the age of the boiler.

According to the newsreel, *Lion* was 'one hundred years old and still going, if not strong, at least going' almost toy-like compared to the blue and silver *Coronation* 'huge and massive, dwarfing her predecessors in both looks and performance'. All over, on Monday 14 June *Lion* was hoisted on board a well-wagon and was despatched to Crewe 'for a wash and brush up', before going back on display at Lime Street. The six coaches returned to Derby for storage.

In the following year, *Lion* took part in the celebrations of the centenary of the LMS at Euston in September 1938. Prior to this appearance, *Lion* was sent for inspection at

Crewe and the opportunity was taken to pose her next to the as-yet-unpainted *Duchess of Hamilton*. A photograph of the unusual couple appeared in Yorkshire newspapers. From Crewe she was transported to London on a railway wagon (minus chimney) in the company of another LNWR veteran, *Cornwall,* and the LNWR replica of *Rocket.* The *Birmingham Daily Gazette* thought *Lion*, with her polished-wood boiler cladding, 'presents a striking contrast to the 164-ton streamlined giants of today'. The Euston exhibition was formally opened by the Lord Mayor of Birmingham (Mr E. R. Canning), the Mayor of St Pancras (Mr J. Sperni) and Lord Josiah Stamp, Chairman of the LMS. Amongst the 200 exhibits on display were Furness Railway No. 3 *Coppernob*, Queen Adelaide's Saloon of 1843, Queen Victoria's Saloon of 1869, modern LMS coaching stock, as well as models of Euston and Kilsby Tunnel in 1838. On 20 September *Lion* steamed out of the old departure platform at Euston, followed by the LMS streamliner *Duchess of Gloucester* with Lord Stamp at the controls. The *Leeds Mercury* reported:

> *Lion* of Leeds in Action ... *Lion* the first locomotive built at the Leeds works of Todd, Kitson & Laird was used today at Euston station to illustrate railway progress during the century that has passed since the first through trains ran from London to Birmingham ... *Lion* is believed to be oldest locomotive in the world capable of working a train. As none of the London and Birmingham engines survive, it was chosen to represent the engines of 100 years ago. On the footplate to-day (alongside a driver and fireman wearing long whiskers and the uniforms of a century ago, with Eton jackets and white trousers) was Lieutenant-Colonel E. Kitson Clark, a director of Kitson & Co. of the Airedale Foundry, Leeds, and a grandson of *Lion*'s builder. (*Leeds Mercury,* 20 September 1938)

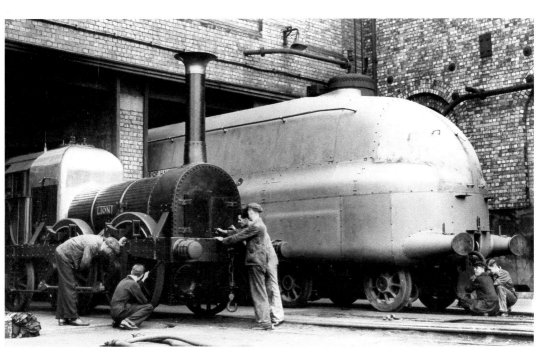

Lion was front-page news in Leeds in 1938 when she was posed at Crewe standing next to the named, but unpainted, *Duchess of Hamilton*. (L&NWR Society)

With her crew attractively attired in period costume, *Lion* roars away from Euston Station as part of the 100th anniversary celebrations.

Lion's visit to Euston also coincided with Colonel Kitson Clark's half-century as a railway engineer, having joined Kitson & Co. on 14 September 1888. Despite his fifty-year association with railways, the *Leeds Mercury* noted he had only twice driven a railway locomotive, one of those occasions being *Lion* in 1930 at Liverpool. Kitson Clark was a forward-thinker and in an interview with the *Mercury* in September 1938 expressed his belief that Leeds would one day be a smokeless city 'that helicopters will one day be a common method of rising out of Leeds, and that one day in Leeds there may not only be no horses but no private cars'. The Euston exhibition was a 'real treat' with *Lion* working short trips with open carriages; the Railway Correspondent of the *Derby Daily Telegraph* opined that 'the old open wagons for passengers are in themselves an argument which confounds all criticism of present day railway accommodation, even on branchlines'. After her London visit, *Lion* was returned to her plinth at Lime Street but in April 1941 was removed for safety to the paint shop at Crewe Works 'as a wartime measure'.

   Lion was next on show to mark the Stephenson Centenary in August 1948, at Chesterfield, where she was on display with the LNWR replica of *Rocket* and Midland Railway single-wheeler No. 673. *Lion* and *Rocket* were transported by rail in an early-morning special movement leaving Crewe at 1.20 am:

VIPs and dignitaries, including Lord Stamp, Chairman of the LMS, assemble on *Lion*'s footplate at Euston.

Lion on display at Euston in September 1938. She stood in marked contrast to the LMS streamliner on the opposite platform.

Colonel E. Kiston Clark, grandson of James Kitson (the builder of *Lion*) who drove *Lion* in 1930 in Liverpool and in 1938 at Euston.

Lion attended the celebrations held in Chesterfield to mark the centenary of the death of George Stephenson.

The train will include special wagons on which will be loaded a full-scale model of the 'Rocket' and the '*Lion*' locomotive ... and an 1842 coach built for Queen Adelaide. This coach will run on its own wheels. At Derby the train will pick up Queen Victoria's saloon coach, two old locomotives, a modern corridor coach, and a shock-absorbing wagon loaded with specimens of old and new railway track. The train will also include a locomotive of the London Midland region 'Patriot' class and latest examples of modern passenger coaches and wagons. (*Derby Daily Telegraph*, 7 August 1948)

In May 1951 *Lion* had her second film part, appearing briefly in *The Lady with the Lamp*, a biopic of Florence Nightingale, and in so doing renewed her acquaintance with Anna Neagle, who played Nightingale, and Michael Wilding, appearing as Sidney Herbert. Made by British Lion films and directed by Herbert Wilcox, it was premiered in October of that year. *Lion* left Crewe works on 29 May for Cole Green, Hertfordshire, where the railway scenes were filmed, despite the disparity between an 1838 locomotive and carriages appearing in a film set in 1855. But as the set director explained, 1855 rolling stock was scarce and *Lion* and her coaches were sufficiently Victorian.

As part of the Festival of Britain of 1951 *Lion* returned to Liverpool and was on show at Liverpool Exchange station from 22 July to 11 August 1951. Here she was joined with fellow veteran *Coppernob*, Queen Adelaide's saloon and Queen Victoria's saloon.

Thunderbolts from Titfield

Lion is perhaps best known for her role as the titular *Thunderbolt* in the 1953 hit Ealing comedy *The Titfield Thunderbolt* – written by T. E. B. Clarke and based on the adventures of L. T. C. Rolt and his band of volunteers reviving the Tal-Y-Llyn railway in North Wales. The film tells the story of a plucky band of villagers led by the Vicar (Rev. Sam Weech (George Relph)) and Squire (John Gregson), who attempt to save their railway from closure by BR and competition from the local bus company of Pearce & Crump. Directed by Charles Crichton, it was filmed over eight weeks in summer 1952 on the closed Limpley Stoke–Camerton branch near Bath, with Monkton Combe becoming Titfield and Bristol Temple Meads Mallingford. The Limpley Stoke–Camerton branch of the GWR had been opened in 1910 primarily for coal traffic. It ran for most of its length alongside the Somerset Coal Canal, but due to the collieries which served the line closing, the branch saw its last train on 14 February 1951. The Limpley Stoke–Camerton line had previously been used to film *The Ghost Train* (1931) by Arnold Ridley (who would later play Private Godfrey in *Dad's Army*), and *Kate plus Ten* (1937) at the disused Dunkerton Colliery. Because the branch had been closed for two years, the station building at Monkton Combe was tidied up and given new running-in boards proclaiming 'Titfield'. A dummy home signal was erected 200 yards south of the station and a dummy water crane was also erected. At Dunkerton Colliery sidings a picturesque occupation crossing and an adjacent cottage were built by the film makers, and it was here that the Titfield train did battle with a steamroller driven by Harry Hawkins (Sid James) – the roller CH3282 was a 1904 10 hp Aveling & Porter, which has happily survived into preservation.

To prepare her for her role, *Lion* was overhauled at Crewe and the opportunity was also taken to check and calibrate both safety valves to hopefully prevent any further nuisance from blowing off during filming. She was taken to Westbury on a low-loader where she

Monkton Combe in GWR days. It was used to film Arnold Ridley's *The Ghost Train*, and most famously appeared as Titfield in the *Titfield Thunderbolt*.

'caused quite a sensation'. Here *Lion* was repainted into a rather garish livery of bright red and green and underwent a steam test. Although taken to Westbury by road, she ran the final 20 miles to join the film unit on location under her own power, driven by Sydney Mitchell, 'a railwayman of long experience' who expressed 'great satisfaction with the performance of *Lion*, and admiration of the excellent craftsmanship of its makers'.

In addition to *Lion*, two GWR 14XX class 0-4-2 tank locos were used: No. 1401 for film purposes and No. 1456 as bank engine as the 'going was as little heavy for the *Lion* on the gradients of 1 in 100 between Limpley Stoke and Combe Hay, when hauling the train of about 90 tons'. Both engines were supplied by Westbury shed with drivers S. Mitchell and E. Burridge driving *Lion* and No. 1401; Mitchell also appeared (appropriately costumed) in long shots as the double for George Relph. F. Green was his fireman. No. 1456 was driven by drivers H. S. Harris, A. J. King and W. Copeland. Rolling stock for the film was acquired from various locations: an old Wisbech & Upwell tramcar, two GWR brake vans (one of which was fitted up with a diesel-electric 300-amp generator for the arc lamps) and, from Westbury shed, a cattle truck and several conflats, one of which eventually carried 'Dan's cottage'. On 15 June this peculiar train consisting of No. 1456, the Wisbech & Upwell coach, GWR cattle wagon and brake van, arrived at Monkton Combe. *Lion* arrived on set four days later. The Wisbech & Upwell coach used in the filming is now preserved at the North Norfolk Railway. Sadly, neither No. 1401 nor No. 1456 survived into preservation.

As had been discovered during the filming of *Victoria the Great*, *Lion* was prone to blowing-off at inopportune moments. Lack of a damper to control the burn of the fire and a proper pressure gauge made this task even more difficult for the poor fireman, so *Lion* returned to Westbury to be fitted with a pressure gauge and a somewhat crude front damper welded up from chequer plate. Another problem encountered with *Lion* was lighting up: she has no blower to help draw the fire and when cold could take hours to raise steam. The fire would die down when standing stationary, but as soon as she began to move the draw from the blast pipe would revive the fire and the boiler pressure would suddenly come round to blowing-off point and stay there for the rest of the day! Furthermore, the only way of putting water back into the boiler was via the axle-driven feed pumps, so there was no way of calming her down with the judicious use of injectors. Ted Burridge, a BR 'crack express driver', was 'called in' to show George Relph and Sir Godfrey Tearle (Ollie Mathews, Bishop of Westchester and volunteer fireman) how to drive her – or in the words of the newsreel, 'how not to blow her up'. Tearle would die in June 1953, only months after the film was released. A British Pathé newsreel that was made of the filming process made much of *Lion*'s 'star quality', 'the crew finding her as full of fire as an ageing film star' who threatened to 'steal the show from Naunton Wayne [George Blakeworth the Town Clerk] and Stanley Holloway [Walter Valentine, the wealthy benefactor].'

Still carrying her own nameplates, *Lion* stands in her garish *Thunderbolt* garb, in June 1953. (Ivo Peters Collection/ Julian Peters)

Thunderbolt and her oddball train captured by Ivo Peters during filming in summer 1953. (Ivo Peters Collection/ Julian Peters)

One of the key moments of *Titfield Thunderbolt* was having to refill the boiler from the nearby stream following sabotage of the water tower. In fact, the water tower was completely fake: water was indeed taken from the stream, using a diesel pump which can be seen in the background. (Ivo Peters Collection/Julian Peters)

The vehicles used for filming purposes consisted of two GWR 'Toad' brakevans; former Wisbech & Upwell Coach, 'Dan's Cottage' carried on a war-well, and a variety of flat wagons for carrying filming equipment. A trusty 14XX tank engine was in film during each day of filming to shunt stock about and – out of shot – give *Lion* a bit of a push. (Ivo Peters Collection/Julian Peters)

The *Liverpool Echo* (4 April 1953) proudly announced:

> Grand Old Lady of Liverpool becomes a Star After 115 years! ... 'She' is the old Liverpool engine, *Lion*, the oldest working engine in the world, which has the title role in the British film 'The Titfield Thunderbolt' ... Of course she had to be groomed for the part ... so her dark green ... was changed to the shades all the best veteran engines are wearing this Coronation season – nursery red and green. A facial was also necessary for the removal of the nameplate and the substitution of one bearing the terrifying name 'Thunderbolt' ... Otherwise her trim lines remain a joy to the locomophile – and the film publicists to whom she might be another Marilyn Monroe ... It is the *Lion*'s film.

Over the Pennines in Leeds, the Yorkshire press similarly extolled the film-star qualities of *Lion* – and made much of her Yorkshire origin – although the *Yorkshire Evening Post* was less than enamoured with the film itself, commenting that it was 'lacking pace and momentum' and not being all that funny. It was, however, 'worth anyone's money for the cool, serene greenness of the English countryside, in restrained yet appealing colour' – *Thunderbolt* was Ealing's first colour film.

On Shed at Rugby

Lion's final fling before the cameras came in 1961. On 18 October of that year she was filmed on the Rugby–Leamington Branch at Dunchurch for A.T.V.'s 'Look Around' programme, broadcast on 3 November. She was shedded at Rugby and her crew turned out in period-appropriate attire. Her fireman was Fred Oliver, who lived in Marlborough Road, Rugby. When asked how it was to fire *Lion*, Fred replied in the colourful idiom of the footplate, and complained there were no brakes and it was difficult to tell the steam pressure. From Rugby, *Lion* once again returned to Crewe. In 1965 the City of Liverpool Museums approached the surviving trustees who cared for *Lion* with a view to her being put on display in the new transport gallery of the rebuilt museum, where she was installed in 1967.

Upon arrival she was not in the best condition. She had been quickly repainted for her role in the *Titfield Thunderbolt* and then restored to her 1929 livery, but that paint had been applied directly over the varnish applied for *Thunderbolt*. The paint was deteriorating, which would become a serious problem if left untreated. The boiler lagging was in equally poor condition, whilst the coupling rods and motion were rather rusty. Therefore, the decision was made for a cosmetic restoration between 1968 and August 1969. During this process the decision was made to take *Lion*, where possible, 'back to metal', removing a layer of paint almost 1/8-inch thick as well as copious amounts of white lead filler. The decision was made by the museum to repaint *Lion* without resorting to the use of filler. The final topcoat was a specially mixed pigment-dense emerald green which had been darkened to Brunswick green and finished with a semi-matt varnish. Exposed metalwork was waxed to prevent oxidation. Despite the new transport gallery being considered her final home, *Lion* would only reside there for the best part of a decade.

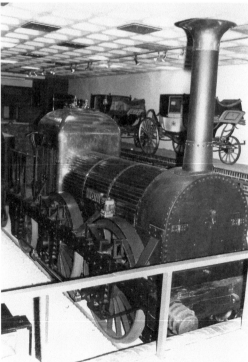

Above: *Lion* was in front of the cameras again in 1961 for ATV, with her crew turned out in period finery. (OLCO)

Left: *Lion* formed the centrepiece of the Transport Gallery in the old Museum of Liverpool.

Chapter 4

Rainhill Renaissance

The Rainhill Trials were a seminal moment in the history of Britain's railways, finally showing the superiority of the steam locomotive over the horse- or rope-worked railways. Whilst the centenary of the event (1929) had not been marked, railway enthusiasts, and indeed British Rail, were eager to mark the 150th anniversary of that world-changing moment. Success of the celebrations surrounding the 150th anniversary of the Stockton & Darlington Railway in 1975 had shown such an event was practical and indeed popular. The late Mike Satow and a team of engineers and historians had built a working replica of *Locomotion No. 1*, which sowed the seed for having replicas of all three Rainhill contestants – *Rocket*, *Sans Pareil*, and *Novelty* – in steam for the big day, which was to be held from 24–26 May 1980 at Bold Colliery, near Rainhill, in Lancashire. At the opposite end of the line, at Liverpool Road station (the original Manchester terminus of the Liverpool & Manchester Railway), the Liverpool Road Station Society organised a grand Railway Exposition during that summer.

Thoughts automatically turned to *Lion* as the only surviving locomotive from the Liverpool & Manchester Railway. This process began as early as 1976, with quotations for the necessary boiler work being received from various boilermakers including Dorothea Restorations Ltd., Rustons Diesels, and National Vulcan Engineering, for the necessary insurance, as well as British Rail. Ultimately, *Lion* was sent to Rustons at Newton-le-Willows, the company which occupied the historic Vulcan Foundry that had been founded in 1832 by Charles Tayleur and Robert Stephenson. The opportunity was taken to use the restoration of *Lion* to working order as a training scheme for apprentices at Rustons, initially under the leadership of Trevor Bates. Trevor had started at Vulcans as an apprentice in the Vulcan Training School in 1965, and then worked for Vulcans until 2002. Given their links to the Liverpool & Manchester and to Robert Stephenson, Rustons embraced the 'Rocket 150' event with gusto, even proposing to build a replica of *Tayleur* – the first locomotive to be built there in 1832. The team restoring *Lion* was initially composed of Trevor and six apprentices, but later grew to over forty.

Lion arrived at Rustons 'looking rather incongruous on the back of a Pickfords articulated lorry', on 4 April 1979, and unloaded into the Paint Shop, which had no heating and was freezing cold. The first task was to remove the buffers (replicas made in 1929/1930), but even this presented a problem as the nuts and bolts used to secure them had square heads (modern nuts and bolts are hexagonal). All the nuts, bolts and other fixings were handmade and 'were all slightly different sizes', not just from each other but across the flats as well. Many of these ancient bolts sheared off along old fracture lines or had broken during the dismantling process, further slowing progress. All the boiler cladding, nameplates, splashers and the large brass firebox cover were carefully removed and labelled. During the dismantling process it was found that

Lion preparing to depart from the Museum of Liverpool for Ruston Diesels at Newton-le-Willows. *Lion* was hauled out of the Transport Gallery with the museum's own Burrel traction engine. (Tom Nicholls)

At first the team of apprentices assigned to work on *Lion* was quite small. Standing proudly with their model of *Rocket* are (L–R) Trevor Bates (supervisor), Ian Gravenor, Leonard Tickle, Robin Lear, Keith Rowlinson and Ian Jamieson. (Trevor Bates)

Many minor items such as nuts, bolts, keys, and split pins were damaged, loose, or missing. Many mating parts were incorrectly assembled, some castings were cracked, and the gaskets, seals and packings were perished.

It was also found that parts of the valve gear had been incorrectly reassembled.

Above: *Lion*, minus chimney, looking somewhat incongruous on a low-lowder at Vulcan Foundry in April 1979. (OLCO)

Right: Work on *Lion* took place in the freezing cold Paint Shop; Vulcan apprentices strip the cladding and insulation from the boiler. (Museum of Liverpool)

The Boiler

With the locomotive stripped back to bare metal, the first major task to be undertaken was a complete examination of the boiler and firebox, and this was the main focus of the restoration team. On 4 September 1979 the BR Boiler Inspector carried out an external inspection, but, despite an hour of 'ear-splitting hammering on the external plating and contorted attempts to view the internal condition', it was decided that in order for a full internal examination to take place, the main steam pipe, regulator and boiler tubes would have to be removed, and this, sadly, represented a loss of historic material. Re-tubing of the boiler was also in line with BR's policy for preserved steam locomotives of a re-tube every ten years. In an attempt to reduce the amount of boiler work necessary, and to minimise the damage to or loss of historic material, it was hoped by the Rustons team that non-destructive testing with ultrasonic techniques would be used, but given that Low Moor iron has a tendency to 'segregate' over time, it was thought that this might have given false thickness readings. Thus, the only reliable way of assessing the condition of the boiler barrel was to remove the tubes.

Due to the age of the tubes and the tube plates, the first tube was cut out using a hammer and a half-round chisel (known as a 'fishback'). The chisel was used to cut two slots axially into each tube so that the tube could be pushed through the tube plate using a hydraulic jack. The first tube was thus removed on 14 September 1979, a laborious process which took five hours. Lessons were quickly learned which sped up the process. The slots cut into the ends of the tube had not been cut deep enough and had only been cut to little more than the depth of the tube plate, rather than a recommended 2 inches. Secondly, because copper is fairly soft, as the copper tube was hammered, the metal was peened outwards and formed a constricting ridge around the tube inside the tube plate, which prevented its easy withdrawal. Simply hammering the tube to remove it did not work, so a drift and hydraulic jack were used to force the tube through the tube plate some 3 inches. This was so the chiselled and expanded section of the tube was out of the boiler and then could be easily removed by hand.

Even after a faster working method had been devised, it was still a fairly lengthy process, so the use of oxyacetylene cutting equipment was resorted to, and the first tubes were successfully cut out on 18 September, under close supervision. Sadly, however, when the task was handed over to the apprentices, the smokebox tube plate was damaged in five places. The use of oxyacetylene cutting gear was stopped, and advice sought on how to repair the tube plate, which was successfully repaired using arc welding techniques by a professional welder from the fabrication shop. Each of the damaged holes in the tube plate were filled with weld and then ground down. The whole tube plate was wire brushed and then needle gunned.

Crisis averted, from then on, no tube was to be removed without personal supervision. Eventually, greater confidence and care meant that the thin copper tubes could be burned away before the tube plate itself became hot. Examination of the smokebox tube plate showed that it bowed outwards a full inch (2.2 cm). There was also evidence of a steam leak and wastage in the smokebox, especially around where the steam manifold casting was bolted to the tube plate and around the bottom left-hand side (facing the engine), with the tube plate having lost 1/8 of an inch of material.

There was also evidence that the boiler had been re-tubed in the past as copper ferrules were found in each of the holes in the firebox tube plate and in some of the holes of the smokebox tube plate. These ferrules had been used to reduce the diameter of the tube holes.

Evidence of the damage caused by trying to remove boiler tubes after using oxyacetylene cutting gear. Luckily, the damage to the tube plate was repairable. (Trevor Bates)

A Vulcan apprentice at work in *Lion*'s smokebox. (Trevor Bates)

Lion's front tube plate prior to re-tubing. The construction of the smokebox is readily apparent, the plates of the smokebox being secured to the turned-over edge of the tube plate. (Trevor Bates)

The new tubes were carefully expanded and had their edges turned over to make them watertight. (Trevor Bates)

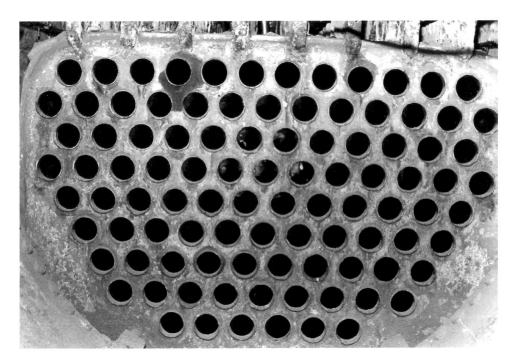

The copper firebox tube plate was heavily worn; copper ferrules had been inserted into each of the tube holes. The crown of the firebox is supported by eight iron girder stays. (Trevor Bates)

Many of the holes in the smokebox tube plate showed signs of wear and varied between 2.0 inches diameter to 2.08 inches diameter 'and all the tubes gave the appearance of being heavily rolled and swaged' at the smokebox end. The same was true in the firebox, where all the tube holes in the copper tube plate had been sleeved with copper, and most of the holes were in fact oval, rather than circular, and had worn to as much as 2.14 inches diameter (from 2.0 inches). Clearly, the engine would have required re-tubing sooner rather than later, as the age of the tubes was uncertain and had probably been replaced by the LMS in 1929–1930. By the end of *Lion*'s career as a pump, steam was fed from an external donkey boiler, suggesting the boiler was then in poor condition and needed extensive work. With the tubes removed attention could now be turned to removing the main steam pipe and regulator assembly, a task, like removing the tubes, which was easier said than done.

Regulator Problems

The removal of the main steam pipe and regulator presented the restoration team with their biggest headache. The main steam pipe is 12 feet long and 5 inches in diameter and is made from rolled arsenical copper that is ¼-inch thick. It is secured to the smokebox tube plate via a cast-brass flange, to which it had been soldered in situ. The steam pipe was secured to the regulator assembly with four 'hook bolts' around a smaller flange. Access to the joint was made problematic due to its cramped location just above the firebox crown sheet.

At the front end, the steam pipe flange was fastened to the tube plate with four large bolts, which, after a liberal application of penetrating oil, could be easily undone. The four 'hook bolts' at the rear end, however, despite having been soaked in penetrating oil for three days, still required 'starting' using a hammer and chisel. These hook bolts were

Looking down through *Lion*'s manhole cover. Prominent is the main steam pipe and the four 'hook bolts' which proved so troublesome to remove to the restoration team. (Trevor Bates)

extremely difficult to reach; one poor apprentice had to work quite literally 'standing on his head' working through the manhole on top of the firebox! The two lower bolts were easily removed, despite the cramped access, but due to the bolts being handmade, with each of the 'flats' having different sizes, they required the use of two spanners to unfasten the nuts. These bolts 'nocked out of the flange relatively easily' but because the flange was stepped (unknown to the restoration team at that time) there was 'no movement ... at the flange joint when sideways pressure was applied'.

The next piece to be removed was the 'T' shaped steam manifold, which branches left and right to supply steam to the cylinders. This was secured by four nuts, threaded on to studs, which held both it and the cast-brass main steam pipe flange in position. Where the studs pass through the flange, they are square and pass through square holes, and are thus prevented from turning and working loose. The flange is actually inserted into the hole drilled through the tube plate from the outside. Two of the nuts were easily removed but the pair at the bottom of the cast had to be started with a hammer and chisel. With all four nuts removed, the flange would not move, 'despite levering with baulks of timber and the use of a car scissor jacket'. The flange and its joint were wire brushed to remove any corrosion products and the joint was soaked with penetrating oil for two days. The flange was finally extracted with the help of a small hydraulic jack!

Next out was the regulator assembly. This is a heavy brass casting, weighing nearly a hundredweight (50 kg), secured to the outer firebox wrapper with six bolts; four short and two long. Each bolt sheared off, in turn, in the brass regulator each time an attempt was made to loosen them – despite being soaked for several days with penetrating oil. The

With the T-shaped steam manifold, which distributed steam to the two cylinders, removed, the end of the main steam pipe can be seen. Sadly, in order to remove the main steam pipe to gain access to the boiler, it had to be cut through and replaced. (Trevor Bates)

broken bolts were retained, and copies were made, but the regulator and steam pipe had still not been removed from the boiler.

Study of the regulator assembly and how it was jointed to the main steam pipe revealed many answers. The stepped, half-flange between the steam pipe and regulator assembly meant that the main steam pipe could be passed into the boiler, through the hole in the front tube plate, and thus marry up with the half-flange at the end of the regulator assembly. It should have been possible to have reversed this process and push the main steam pipe back through the front tube plate. However, it was 'practically impossible to apply force in the correct direction' and, secondly, there was a high risk of damaging the main steam pipe. The main steam pipe and regulator assembly were, in effect, acting as a stay between the front tube plate and the outer firebox wrapper. It must have been a very cramped job for the boiler smith (probably a boy) who had to be physically inside the boiler to secure the main steam pipe to the regulator, as well as to solder it to the flange at the smokebox end.

The only means of removing the regulator and main steam pipe was, therefore, to separate the steam pipe from its smokebox flange. The decision was made, albeit reluctantly, to cut through the main steam pipe, and this was achieved without any damage to the brass flange. With the main steam pipe and flange out of the boiler, it was soon observed that the soldered joint between it and the flange were 'very poor indeed, and only being obtained over 2/3 the circumference', suggesting that it had never been completely steam-tight. Len Morris (who took charge of the restoration from Trevor Bates) concluded that the joint between the steam pipe and flange had been made via force or friction-fit (the main steam pipe being slightly over size, but also softer than the brass flange), and then the joint soldered up by some poor soul in the boiler shell – no wonder the final result was so poor.

Removal of the steam pipe was managed through using a specially constructed 'extractor' which bolted on the tube plate. The steam pipe was 'lifted until level with the hole in the front boiler plate and slide out … the half flange just fitted through the hole in the boiler plate'. The regulator could then be removed and, with the help of a small hydraulic jack, was lifted out through the manhole in the top of the boiler, again only just fitting through. Where the fixing bolts had snapped off, they were drilled out and re-tapped by apprentices in the training school.

The problems kept mounting up. With the regulator on the bench it was found that the casting was cracked. The regulator is of the 'plug type', with a large brass plunger which is worked in and out to increase or reduce the amount of steam passing into the steam pipe. The regulator handle works in a helical brass guide which 'screws' the regulator in and out. It opens away from the driver (i.e. in an anticlockwise direction). It was hoped that the original casting could be kept, but the decision was taken to have a new regulator cast in October 1979. The original steam pipe was also not reused, and when the boiler was re-tubed it was replaced by a version in steel. The original was kept, and it was hoped it could be repaired and put back into the engine at a later date. The five boiler stays were also removed and, due to severe wastage, were replaced by new examples when the boiler was re-tubed.

With the regulator and main steam pipe out of the now empty boiler shell, it was possible for a slim member of the restoration team to squeeze into the boiler through the manhole and descale the boiler. Several hundredweight of rust, scale and a 'cement-like' deposit was removed with the use of chipping hammers and a needle gun. Wastage of the boiler plates was found to be no more than 1/8-inch, remarkably little for a boiler of its age, but the amount of scale and other deposits showed that it had probably not been washed out since passing through the hands of the LMS in 1929/1930.

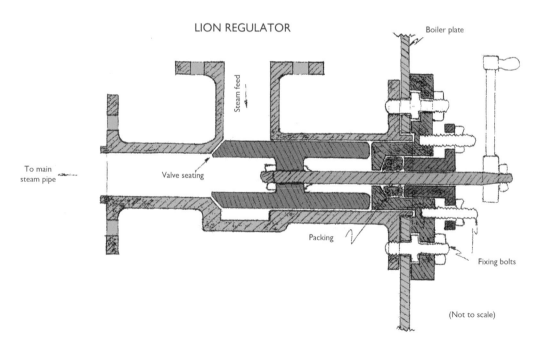

Lion has a 'Crewe-type' regulator (here in cross section) which uses a plug-valve which is worked in and out using a helical regulator quadrant. (Andrew S. Mason)

During the restoration it was found that the original regulator plug-valve was badly cracked, and a replacement was produced by Ruston. (Trevor Bates)

A Ruston apprentice at work in cramped conditions de-scaling the inside of *Lion*'s boiler. (OLCO)

Left: British Railways boiler inspectors examining *Lion*'s boiler before being re-tubed. (OLCO)

Below: A member of the Ruston's team prepares to descend within the boiler barrel. (OLCO)

BR boiler inspectors examining the boiler: a member of Ruston's staff is already inside. (OLCO)

Wheels, Bearings and Buffers

The opportunity was taken to examine the mechanical parts of the locomotive including the valve gear, bearings and the wheels. As with the boiler, cracks and problems were found. The tyres on the cast-iron wheels were found to be loose, especially that on the left-hand leading driving wheel. More significantly, however, that wheel was found to be cracked. This was repaired using the 'Metalock' metal stitching process. This involved sinking dumbbell-shaped keys into the wheel across the line of the crack, which were then expanded into the crack. The tyres, although very worn and passed by the BR inspector, were not amended given that *Lion* was thought to only be making an appearance at Rocket 150. Loose and worn tyres would become a problem later.

One of the gabs was also found to be cracked, but on closer examination this was found to be left over from the original manufacturing process. At some point in her history, *Lion* had also run 'hot' the big-end and its driving axle bearings, having been damaged, needed to be shimmed by 60-thou. Dismantling (and later, reassembling) the complicated valve gear was hampered through 'fag paper' tolerances. Also, many of the components had not been correctly reassembled with tell-tales and witness marks being often confused and contradictory. At some point in their history, the iron wedges which held the big-end assemblies together had been hammered with a hard steel hammer which had resulted in the softer iron wedges 'spreading', making them difficult to remove. The wedges had to be gently filed back to shape and only copper hammers were used during reassembly by the restoration team. The original square-headed nuts and bolts holding the valve gear together had all been handmade, with no one nut or bolt being identical to the next, with 'flats' of

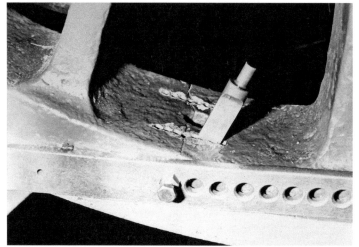

The left-hand leading driving wheel was found to be badly cracked around a tyre bolt hole. It was repaired using the 'Metalock' process, where dumbbell-shaped keys were let into the wheel and then expanded. When filled and ground down the crack was invisible. (Trevor Bates)

Members of Ruston's staff reassembling *Lion*'s valve gear and water pumps. During the reassembly process it was found that many components had a hair-breadth tolerance. (Trevor Bates)

different lengths, and with different torque. Many of them broke along old fatigue cracks during reassembly and the decision was made to replace all fixings with new, modern, hexagonal nuts and bolts, although, during her stay in Manchester (1999–2007), railway volunteer Peter Brown recalled he was tasked with replacing many of these modern fixings with traditional Whitworth square-headed examples.

The front buffer beam is made from a single oak plank; originally it, like the main frames, would have been of 'sandwich' construction. It is severely cracked and had to be strengthened with the judicious use of angle irons. Furthermore, BR stipulated there had to be side chains between the locomotive and tender, and on the locomotive and tender. BR also stipulated that the locomotive be fitted with continuous automatic brakes, and an air-brake system (from a commercial HGV) was fitted to the tender, acting on the existing tender brake gear.

Back in Steam

Lion was hydraulically tested on 11 December 1979 in the presence of the BR inspectors. The boiler was taken to twice its normal working pressure (100 psi) and was able to maintain it without any leaks. The first steam test was held on 13 December. A warming fire had been lit the previous day and pressure was gradually raised over a period of five hours to 40 psi. At 11.30 am on 13 December, *Lion* moved under her own power for the first time in nineteen years. She was, once again, the oldest working railway locomotive in the world. The first trial took place on the 'mainline' at the Vulcan Works, and other than one blowing joint 'everything was perfect'. The *Liverpool Echo* reported that 'nearly 1,000 people turned up at the Vulcan works' on 3 February 1980 to witness *Lion* 'roar back into life'. She was reported as being capable of 45 mph but in the opinion of Len Morris 'we are keeping her down to 20 mph to help preserve her forever'.

On the following day (4 February 1980), *Lion* was despatched to the now defunct Steamport museum at Southport. She travelled from Newton-le-Willows to Prescott Street CM&EE depot, Wigan, on the back of a low-loader, where she was re-railed and 'left locked up for the night' ready for a mainline run from Wigan to Southport under steam. The official BR crew struggled to raise steam. Ignoring the advice of the museum staff they had set about preparing the engine as they would a modern mainline locomotive, but soon discovered there was no blower to help bring the fire round. *Lion* sat at Wigan making an awful lot of yellow smoke but not very much steam until the museum team were allowed onto the footplate. She was given a "tow start' to draw up the fire … [which] persuaded the old lady to go. She steamed sedately out of a crowded yard' after having nearly missed her road. *Lion* can basically be fired like a traction engine, lit up on bits of old wood and rags 'stirred around the grate', producing a volcanic column of dirty black smoke. She will raise steam quite quickly when warm but, from the lack of a blower, when left standing the fire will die down and then suddenly burst into life once she starts to move (and making a lot of black smoke in the process), often leading to her blowing off. *Lion* is very economical, and it can be quite easy to over-fire her.

Lion, back in steam at Ruston's on 13 December 1979. Len Morris, who eventually led the restoration, is wearing the top hat. Evidence of where the leading left-hand wheel rubs against the smokebox can be clearly seen. (Trevor Bates)

Captured for posterity. Following completion, *Lion*'s safety valves lift at 50 psi in February 1980. (OLCO)

Lion in steam on the Ruston's 'mainline' at their historic Vulcan Foundry site, spring 1980. (OLCO)

The museum team didn't know how much water *Lion* would use, nor how much air for the brakes, so a water stop was planned at Burscough Bridge where the Merseyside Fire Brigade Museum's Dennis fire engine provided water, and Adrian Jarvis's Land Rover was also on hand to provide air for the brakes. She steamed into Burscough Bridge to be confronted with school parties, cameras, and 'festoons of gricers'. *Lion* departed Burscough Bridge in the wake of a DMU and ran superbly to Southport, where she ran round the triangle so that she would face the right way for her later trip to Bold Colliery to take part in the Rocket 150 celebrations.

Lion was on the mainline and in steam again on 24 March 1980 to take part in the naming of Class 86 No. 86228, which had been named *Vulcan Heritage* to mark the 150th anniversary of the Vulcan Foundry, established by Charles Tayleur and Robert Stephenson. It had originally been planned to name the locomotive *Vulcan Foundry 1832–1982* with a figure of Vulcan and his anvil, but BR didn't like the idea of private companies being advertised in such a way, so requested the name change to *Vulcan Heritage*. No. 86228 was duly named at Wigan Wallgate with *Lion* in steam in the goods yard. Following the ceremony, the invited guests and VIPs went for lunch and *Lion* ran to Southport on the mainline, taking water at Burscough Bridge sidings, and remaining at Southport until 18 May.

The run to Bold Colliery via Wigan Wallgate was made on Thursday 22 May 1980 with two replica coaches, and without any difficulties. On board was a complement of special VIP passengers who had made the run possible. A water stop was made at Wigan Wallgate, a stop which proved to be unnecessary as *Lion* was only using as little as 15 gallons of water per mile. According to Adrian Jarvis, upon arrival at Bold there were 'about forty

Lion arrives at Burscough Bridge en route to Southport. Here she stopped to take on water (thanks to Merseyside Fire Brigade) and recharged the air brakes.

Lion and her train of period carriages in the yard at Steamport, Southport, in spring 1980.

Making her way to Bold Colliery, *Lion*, together with period rolling stock, returned to the Liverpool & Manchester mainline, probably for the first time since 1859. (Ben Jackson)

men in orange jackets who could tell us what we should not do, but few, if any, who could tell us what we could do' and several frayed tempers. During the fortnight at Bold there were no major incidents, other than on Press Day (23 May 1980), when *Lion* put her nose in the dirt because the track was in such poor condition: the track was found to be 2 ½ inches over gauge. As a result, *Lion* received much publicity for all the wrong reasons. On the following Saturday, *Lion* was making steam to take part in the cavalcade, and was running up and down to warm through and 'blow all the 'nasty' out of the tubes', 'most of which landed on the Advanced Passenger Train, foolishly parked downwind.' *Lion* displayed 'her customary flawless reliability' and was frequently used for shunting duties at Bold Colliery sidings.

From Bold Colliery *Lion* returned to Newton-le-Willows for Ruston's Gala Day on 5 July. The following Monday, *Lion* travelled from Wigan to the Dinting Railway Centre under her own power (7 May 1980), and from Dinting to Manchester to take part in the 'Great Railway Exposition', which was held at Liverpool Road from 2 August to 14 September 1980. On 14 September she was hauled together with three replica coaches from Liverpool Road to Eccles station, which was suitably bedecked with bunting and flags. Here the train was joined by invited guests and a military band and travelled in fine style to Manchester to celebrate the 150th anniversary of Liverpool Road station. Her final tour date of 1980 was at the Birmingham Railway Museum at Tyseley.

The start of the 1981 tour season saw *Lion* being taken to Newton Heath, near Manchester, for a boiler examination. Her first visit of the year was to Dinting, and she also

Lion, with a packed trainload, standing at Bold Colliery in 1980.

Old meets new: *Lion* (from 1838) standing alongside the newest mainline motive power in the shape of the new High-Speed Train (Class 43). Set No. 253034 (of 1979) was on loan from BR Western Region in order to appear in the cavalcade.

Lion made the first of several visits to Manchester in summer 1980 to take part in the 'Great Railway Exposition'.

visited the Worth Valley Railway, running shuttles between Keighley and Ingrow with a single third-class coach, but during the year the number of problems with the engine started to grow. It was being found that the wash-out plugs, even after having their thread re-cut, were not quite steam-tight and did not seat very well. On another occasion, *Lion* fired her whistle several feet into the air (without causing spectators any injury) following the failure of the whistle spigot. The fire was quickly dropped, and she had to be shunted up and down by a diesel shunter with both pumps on to calm things down. There were also problems with the pumps and clack valves, and the drawbar was also found to be working loose. Three other problems were far more serious: worn tyres and a loose tyre, which had never been properly attended to in 1930, and a crack in the right-hand cylinder end cover, where it supported the slide bars. The decision was made therefore to withdraw *Lion* from steam in 1984, having last steamed at the Science Museum Store at Wroughton. Repair of the cracked cylinder end cover presented Adrian Jarvis and the Liverpool Museum team with an ethical dilemma as to how to proceed. Eventually a process using Sifbronze was chosen because it could be easily reversed. But this was one of an increasing list of problems with the engine simply due to its age.

Standing at platform 3 at Keighley station, *Lion* made several appearances on the Worth Valley Railway in the early 1980s.

Whilst visiting the Worth Valley, *Lion* and a single open carriage ran shuttles between Keighley and Ingrow.

150th Birthday Parties

In June 1984 a group of like-minded enthusiasts held the first meeting of a reconstituted 'Old Locomotive Committee'. Mindful of *Lion*'s upcoming 150th anniversary, OLCO put forward suggestions to help mark that event. Part of OLCO's remit was also to encourage research into the locomotive as well as act as a 'support crew' for the locomotive on its steaming days around the country. With *Lion* no longer in steamable condition, OLCO nowadays concentrates on model engineering, as well as still encouraging research into the locomotive.

Between 1984 and 1987 *Lion* remained on static display in Liverpool, but to mark the 150th anniversary of the opening of the Grand Junction Railway, *Lion* was put back into steam to attend celebrations in Crewe in July 1987. This coincided with the opening of the Crewe Heritage Centre, on 24 July 1987, by HM Queen Elizabeth II. She was at Crewe until August 1987 and then was resident at Dinting Railway Centre until May 1988. Whilst at Dinting, the opportunity was taken to re-tyre the leading wheelset. For this work to take place the valve gear and connecting rods were taken down and *Lion* was gently lifted off her wheels using a large crane. New tyres were made by Krupps of Germany and fitted by Hunslets of Leeds, whose staff worked in 'near arctic conditions' over the winter of 1988–1989 at Dinting. The removed original tyre underwent metallurgical analysis, which showed it to have been made from Low Moor iron, dating it to before *c.* 1860. A retaining bolt was also analysed and also shown to be Low Moor iron. The tyre itself was marked 'Crewe', suggesting it had been fitted by the LNWR at Crewe Works, which had started rolling tyres in 1855.

Other work carried out at Dinting included ultrasonic testing of *Lion*'s boiler in August 1989 by McEwans, which noted wastage on the copper inner firebox. McEwans had, in

Lion celebrated her 150th birthday with style. She was present at the opening of the Crewe Heritage Centre in 1987 and again in 1988.

1988, copper welded some star cracks around the firebox stay heads, which had threatened to cancel the planned operating days that year. The non-destructive test also showed wastage on the boiler shell around the firehole door, but the tubes (from 1979) were 'as new'.

During 1988 *Lion* was steamed on thirty-eight occasions – by far the highest number in preservation. However, 1988 would be her final year in operation. After a birthday party in Southport, in July and August 1988 she was at Tyseley, at Wroughton in September, and rounded off the season at Manchester before returning to Tyseley in November. Janet Ford, a member of the reconstituted OLCO remembers how 'the two visits by 'Lion' to Birmingham Railway Museum produced some record crowds at Tyseley' with 10,000 visitors coming to see *Lion* during her ten-day-long visit. Sadly, *Lion* has not returned to Leeds, the city of her 'birth', since 1838, despite Colonel Kitson Clark suggesting in *c*. 1929 that she should return, and a request being made in 1981 for *Lion* to take part in a cultural festival in Leeds.

Following the anniversary celebrations, the decision was taken that *Lion* should no longer be steamed; she was increasingly tired and running the engine was becoming a serious

Driven by Ray Sharples, *Lion* moves off from the platform at the Museum of Science & Industry, Manchester, October 1988. Manchester was the penultimate stop on her 150th birthday year tour.

drain on Liverpool Museums and its staff. Furthermore, in 1990 her ten-yearly 'boiler ticket' expired and *Lion* would have to be re-tubed. It was hoped *Lion* would be moved to the Museum of Science & Industry in Manchester for this work to take place. Instead of travelling to Manchester, *Lion* headed to Derbyshire to Dorothea Restorations of Whaley Bridge, in July 1991, to assess the condition of the locomotive and whether it was possible, or desirable, for *Lion* to return to steam. This was the result of an agreement between Liverpool Museums and sponsorship from British Coal, who generously funded the cost of the exploratory work. Whilst at Dorothea, *Lion* was turned over on compressed air and 'ran like clockwork'. Sadly, the cost of restoring *Lion* to steaming condition was far above the means of the Museum, the result of which led to meetings between OLCO, the Transport Trust and Liverpool Museums to investigate means of funding this work. Finally, in February 1994 the Board of Trustees of Liverpool Museums decided that *Lion* would not be restored to steam, recognising the high percentage of historic fabric that the locomotive possessed and that any future restoration would result in destruction of such fabric, and continued operation of the locomotive would also result in further loss of historic material. She would undergo a period of conservation to prevent any further deterioration of her condition.

This was in order to preserve and conserve *Lion* for the enjoyment of future generations of railway enthusiasts and students of locomotive and engineering history. Thus, *Lion* was cosmetically restored at Dorothea (although not repainted) and the boiler tubes and main steam pipe, which dated from 1979, were removed. The boiler was found to be in reasonable condition, but there was some wastage and pitting (as noted earlier by McEwans) and one of the cylinder bores was found to be severely pitted for most of its length. Repairing this would have necessitated the cylinder re-boring and sleeving, or a new cylinder casting. *Lion* returned to Liverpool and went on display in Spring 1995.

Whilst the new Museum of Liverpool was being built, *Lion* was resident at MOSI (Manchester) from 1999 to 2007. In 2005 she was a popular exhibit at the 'Riot of Steam' event held at MOSI to mark the 175th anniversary of the Liverpool & Manchester Railway. It was perhaps the then largest gathering of 1830s locomotives, with operational replicas of *Planet* as well as the three Rainhill contenders (*Rocket, Novelty, Sans Pareil*) also in steam. Also present was the 1928 Science Museum-built replica of *Novelty*, which incorporates the original wheels and one cylinder.

Following an inspection by Liverpool Museums staff in 2006, and reception of a report by Jim Rees of the National Railway Museum, *Lion* underwent a £6,019 cosmetic restoration in order to prepare her for display in the new museum. *Lion* was in poor external condition and was two different shades of green: the tender tank had been stripped back to metal and repainted in 1979 with Ruston's in-house green whilst the wheels and wheel splashers were a lighter shade. The bottom of the tender tank was corroding; the boiler cladding was bulging and splitting, and the frames showed signs of pitting. The tender tank was

A rather forlorn-looking *Lion* standing at Dorothea Restorations, awaiting the outcome of whether she was to return to steam. (OLCO)

Lion stands proudly outside the 'Power Hall' at MOSI, Manchester, where she was on loan from 1999 to 2007. (David Boydell)

'Riot of Steam' in 2005 was perhaps the largest gathering of 1830s steam locomotives in the world. *Lion* took a prominent role alongside replicas of *Rocket* and Sans *Pareil*. (David Boydell)

stripped back to metal and filled and repainted, as were the wheels. The splashers were also repainted. The frames and smokebox were cleaned, and the motion was dismantled, cleaned and treated with linseed oil.

Lion now takes pride of place in the Great Port gallery in the visually striking Museum of Liverpool, which opened on 19 July 2011. In 2012 *Lion* was presented with the Heritage Engineering Award by the Institute of Mechanical Engineers – a fitting tribute to those who have worked so hard to preserve, restore and conserve *Lion* for future generations to enjoy.

Shunted by the former Bolton power station Dick, Kerr battery-electric shunter, *Lion* is prepared for road haulage. Taken on 27 February 2007. (David Boydell)

Away she goes! *Lion* all wrapped-up for transport back to Liverpool for cosmetic restoration and display at the new Museum of Liverpool. (David Boydell)

Forming the centrepiece of the 'Great Port' gallery at the Museum of Liverpool, *Lion* is a beloved and ever-popular exhibit. (Ian Hardman)

How Much of
Lion Is 'Original'?

The question of 'originality' of many of *Lion*'s components has been raised since she was recovered in 1928. Firstly, it has to be stated that the locomotive (as preserved) corresponds to no known historical dimensions, other than the wheels of the locomotive named *Lion* running on the Liverpool & Manchester Railway. This suggests either the rebuild of April 1841 was sufficiently major as to leave nothing left of the original, or that the preserved locomotive is in fact not *Lion*. Returning to the question of 'originality', if by that we mean from when *Lion* was built in 1838, then probably very little; perhaps the driven wheels and carrying wheels (the leading wheels are different), but not necessarily the axles. Having flat spokes rather than tubular would be unusual in the 1830s, suggesting they may be later replacements. The wheels are not a good fit; they run extremely close to the smokebox and the clearance between the boiler feed pipe and the left-hand leading wheel has been created by denting the feed pipe at the required point, suggesting they are later replacements. Clearly, the cylinders have been changed (originally 11 × 20 inches), necessitating a change in crank axle to accommodate the shortened stroke/crank throw. The pistons are of late 1830s/early 1840s construction and probably correspond with the change in valve gear. The valve gear is of a type developed in 1840 and thus fits perfectly with the rebuilding in April 1841. The frames are perhaps from 1838, but more likely from 1841, as the original (1838) boiler was considerably shorter than that now carried. The present boiler probably dates from 1865, although it may have been replaced, or at least heavily repaired, around 1900. The copper firebox cladding dates from 1930, as do the wheel splashers, springs, footplate, cab railings, and chimney, which replaced the wrought-iron riveted original. The tender is entirely a product of the LMS using old Furness Railway components. Thus, the 'core' of the locomotive – the boiler and mechanical components – are from 1865 or earlier and are the product of *Lion*'s working life as a locomotive. So, whilst little to none of *Lion* is 182 years old, she is still a grand old lady of 155.

Locomotive	1838	As Preserved
Driving Wheel Diameter	5 ft	5ft
Carrying Wheel Diameter	3ft 6in	3ft 6in
Wheelbase	Unknown	6ft + 6ft
Cylinders	11 x 20 inches	14 x 18 inches
Valve Gear	Melling, Radial	Buddicom, Gab
Valves	Slide	Slide
Valve Area	Unknown	30 sq. inches
Valve Lead	Unknown	3 /32 in
Valve Lap	Unknown	13/16 in
Port Opening	Unknown	1 3/32 in
Valve Travel	Unknown	3 13/16 in
Cut Off	c.80%	81%
Boiler Length	7ft 4in	8ft ½ in (inside)
Boiler Diameter	39 x 42 in	40 ½ in (inside diameter)
Number of Tubes	126	98
Tube Diameter	1 5/8 in (outside diam)	2 in (outside diam)
Tube Length	8ft	8ft 6in
Inner Firebox	30 x 39 in	39 ¾ in x 40 ¾ in
Heating Surface (Tubes)	430.54 sq. ft	447 sq. ft
Heating Surface (Firebox)	39.78 sq. ft	70.5 sq. ft
Heating Surface (Total)	470.32 sq. ft	517.5 sq. ft
Boiler Pressure	50 psi	50 psi
Overall Length	Unknown	23 ft 11 ½ in
Weight (Engine)	14t 9cwt 2qr	18 t 17 cwt
Weight (Leading wheels)	Unknown	6t 16cwt
Weight (Driven Axle)	Unknown	8t 10cwt
Weight (Carry wheels)	Unknown	3t 11 cwt

Tender		
Tender Wheels	Unknown	3ft 6in
Tender Wheelbase	Unknown	5ft
Tender Weight	Unknown	7t 14 cwt
Weight (Leading wheels)	Unknown	3t 6cwt
Weight (Trailing wheels)	Unknown	4t 8 cwt
Overall Length	Unknown	6 ft 11 ½ in

Bibliography

Liverpool Archives
MP/9/2 Proceedings of the Mersey Docks & Harbour Board, Minutes 1859–1860.
MP/9/33 Proceedings of the Mersey Docks & Harbour Board, Minutes 1921–1927.
MP/9/34 Proceedings of the Mersey Docks & Harbour Board, Minutes 1927–1935.
MP/12/7 Mersey Docks & Harbour Board, Docks Committee, Minutes 1872–1875.
MP/12/29 Mersey Docks & Harbour Board, Docks Committee, Minutes 1927–1935.
MP/17/1 Mersey Docks & Harbour Board, Works Committee, Minutes 1858–1860.
MP/17/7 Mersey Docks & Harbour Board, Works Committee,
WUP100/1 Mersey Docks & Harbour Board, coke and coal estimates.

Liverpool Museum
File 1637.41 Locomotive 'Lion'. Miscellaneous notes and papers *c.* 1980–2017.

University of London, Senate House Library
MS 584 (xix), Charles Lawrence Collection, Mss. Letter from Edward Woods to Charles Lawrence, 16 December 1842.

The National Archives, London
RAIL 371/10 Liverpool & Manchester Railway, Management Sub-Committee, Minutes 1833–1839.
RAIL 371/5 Liverpool & Manchester, Board of Directors, Minutes, 1838–1842.
RAIL 371/40 Performances of locomotives and coke consumption, 1839–1840.
RAIL 371/42 Extracts from Liverpool & Manchester and Grand Junction Railway minutes.
RAIL 1007/356 File, 'Lion' Locomotive.

The National Railway Museum, York
MEL/ John Melling Papers.
MEL/1 Letters patent granted to John Melling.
MEL/2 Names and numbers of Liverpool & Manchester locomotives to January 1837.
MEL/3 List of locomotives fitted with 'patent gear' and 'old hand gear', 10 April 1839.
MEL/4 Note, number of locomotives built with patent gearing.

Primary Printed
Anon, 'Specification of Patent granted to John Melling', *The Repertory of Patent Inventions 1838*, new series, vol. X (July -December 1838) (London: J. S. Hodson, 1838).
D. K. Clark, *Railway Machinery: A Treatise on the Mechanical Engineering of Railways* vol. 1 (London: Blackie & Son, 1855).

Z. Colburn, *Locomotive Engineering and the Mechanism of Railways* (London: William Collins, Sons, & Co., 1871).

F. Whishaw, *The Railways of Great Britain and Ireland* 1st edition (London: Simpkin, Marshall & Co, 1840).

E. Woods, 'On Certain Forms of Locomotive Engines', *American Railroad Journal and Mechanics' Magazine*, vol. VIII (1839), pp. 376–379.

E. Woods, 'Expansion of Steam in Locomotives', *The Artizan*, vol. I (1844), pp. 57–60.

E. Woods, 'The Consumption of Fuel in the Locomotive Engine', in *Quarterly Papers on Engineering*, Vol. II (1844), pp. 1–21.

E. Woods, 'On the Consumption of Fuel and the Evaporation of Water in Locomotive and other Steam Engines,' in T. Tredgold, ed., *The Principles and Practice … of Locomotive Engines* (London: John Weale, 1851), pp. 1–44.

Secondary – Books

E. K. Clark, *Kitsons of Leeds 1837–1937* (London: The Locomotive Publishing Co., 1938).

A. L. Dawson, *The Early Railways of Leeds* (Stroud: Amberley Books, 2017).

A. L. Dawson, *Locomotives of the Liverpool & Manchester Railway* (Barnsley: Pen & Sword transport, forthcoming).

A. E. Jarvis, *Prince's Dock* (Liverpool: National Museums and Galleries Merseyside, 1991).

N. Ritchie-Noakes, *Liverpool's Historic Waterfront* (London: HMSO, 1984).

Secondary – Papers and Articles

Anon, 'Links in the History of the Locomotive. No. XV', *The Engineer* (28 December 1883), pp. 500–501.

Anon, 'Links in the History of the Locomotive. No. XIX', *The Engineer* (6 February 1885), pp. 95–97.

Anon, 'An Eighty-year-Old Locomotive' *Locomotive, Railway Wagon & Carriage* Review, vol. 29 (15 January 1923), p. 10.

Anon, 'A Veteran Locomotive Still at Work' *The Locomotive* (15 January 1923).

Anon, 'The Lion Locomotive', *The Engineer* (14 November 1930), p. 535.

Anon, 'The Liverpool & Manchester Railway 0-4-2 *Lion* in the news again', *Journal of the Stephenson Locomotive Society* (November 1961), p. 346.

'R.A.A.', 'The Lion', *LMS Magazine* (August 1937), p. 409.

E. L. Ahrons, 'Short histories of famous firms No. XVII: Kitson & Co', *The Engineer* (12 November 1923), pp. 548–550.

'W.E.S.B.', 'A veteran of the Line', *Locomotive Magazine* (15 January 1829), p. 32.

R. Honri, 'Filming "The Titfield Thunderbolt"', *The Railway Magazine* (March 1953), pp. 163–167

A. E. Jarvis, 'Untwisting the Lion's Tale', *Railway World* (January 1980), pp. 21–24

C. G. Maggs, 'Filming the Titfield Thunderbolt', *The Meccano Magazine*, pp. 338–339.

L. E. Morris, 'The Restoration of 'Lion", *The Railway Magazine* (May 1980), pp. 245–251.

C. W. Reed, 'A Historic Locomotive in use as a pumping engine', *The Railway Magazine* (March 1932), pp. 206–207.

C. W. Reed, 'The Resurrection of the old Lion', *The Railway World* (June 1953), pp. 129–130.

C. W. Reed, 'The Iron 'Lion' Locomotive – Pump Engine – Film Star', *Journal of the Stephenson Locomotive Society* (October 1957), pp. 312–316.

P. W. Shelton, E. F. Clark, P. Heward, J. K. Almond, 'Metallurgical Analysis of the Tyre of Lion Locomotive' ,*Transactions of the Newcomen Society*, vol. 73 (2001–2002), pp. 71–94.

Old Locomotive Committee
Back-copies of newsletter 'Lionsheart' specifically years 1983–1995.
Ruston Diesels '*Lion* Operators Manual' (1980).
Ruston Diesels *Lion* restoration notes.